Chicken Soup and Other Nostrums

Chicken Soup and Other Nostrums

Ted Boadway MD

Illustrated by Joe Weissmann

CBC Enterprises

Montréal • Toronto • London • New York

Copyright © 1987 Canadian Broadcasting Corporation
Illustrations © 1987 Joe Weissmann

Published by CBC Enterprises/Les Entreprises Radio-Canada, a division of the Canadian
Broadcasting Corporation, P.O. Box 500, Station A, Toronto, Ontario M5W 1E6.

Canadian Cataloguing in Publication Data

Boadway, Ted, 1945-
Chicken soup and other nostrums

ISBN 0-88794-327-6

1. Medical delusions. 2. Folk medicine. I. CBC
Enterprises. II. Title.

R133.B63 1987   615.8'8   C87-094411-8

Editor: Ex Libris/Charis Wahl
Design: The Dragon's Eye Press
Electronic Typesetting: Allen Shechtman, CBC Enterprises

Cover illustration: Copyright © Gary Larson
"The Far Side" cartoon is reprinted by permission of
Chronicle Features, San Francisco.

Distributed to the trade by
McClelland and Stewart, Toronto

Printed and bound in Canada by John Deyell Company
1 2 3 4 5 6 / 92 91 90 89 88 87

To Nancy, Kajer, Tobi and Joshua

Who are real to me, and that's no myth

Contents

CONTENTS

Introduction

The way people understand medicine colours the way they tell their stories to doctors when something is bothering them, and influences the way they accept treatment.

This first came to my attention when I did a six-month stint at a church-run hospital in the bush of northern Nigeria shortly after graduating from medical school. After a "terribly cold night" by local standards (at 70° F it was the first comfortable night's sleep I'd had since we arrived) everyone who showed up at the clinic with some complaint blamed it on the weather. *Everything* from obstructed labour to meningitis and malaria was ascribed by the patients to "the cold."

As I listened to these stories, I chuckled to myself. When you are armed with a modern pharmacopoeia, it's easy – too easy – to dismiss any deviation as myth and superstition. But it made me realize how many times I've heard patients back home make similar attempts to explain what's ailing them. The stories the Nigerians told were not different in quantity or quality from other stories I had heard. They were simply different stories.

This got me thinking about medical myths. I have spent a lot of time over the years listening to people who used stories founded in folklore and custom to help describe their complaints. Sometimes the patients didn't even believe the stories, but they would trot them out as a way to begin the conversation. Even the most educated patients relied on these so-called "old wives' tales" to help them explain their problem.

Are carrots good for your eyes? Is a red nose the sign of a drunkard? Will sleeping on a hard bed help a backache? Can chicken soup cure *everything*? There's a germ of truth in some of our cherished folklore. Some of it is pure bunk, but harmless. And some of it can make a bad condition worse.

The interesting thing, I discovered, is that myths change. People's sophistication and medical knowledge has undoubtedly improved over the years. Some of the common old myths, like the one about toads giving you warts, are based on false science and everyone has realized they are false — if a patient brings it up at all, it's usually as a joke. But there are new myths forming all the time. Pre-Menstrual Syndrome is one example that's based on today's science. It has become a buzzword people accept with some readiness as an explanation of all that ails womankind.

I started on the myth-debunking beat when I was asked by Neil Sandell, a radio producer at the Canadian Broadcasting Corporation, to come up with an idea for a regular series. We started working on it and realized, to our amazement, how many folk tales are out there on the tip of everyone's tongue.

The process carried over into my regular work as an information officer for the Ontario Medical Association. It's part of my job to answer public inquiries about disease, new cures and therapies. I found that simply saying a myth isn't true wasn't helpful, but I could use a discussion of the myth to develop communication between doctor and patient.

The first purpose of this book is to look at myths that determine the ways we try to avoid getting sick or "cure" ourselves when we do. We can't simply blame old wives' tales for all our medical mistakes — a few of these myths are so credible that even doctors believe them. But I hope to be able to separate fact from fiction to give you a better understanding of what good health is all about. Knowing where a superstition comes from or how a myth was created is often the key to good medicine.

My second purpose, by no means less important, is to have a bit of fun. Medicine, although it is very serious, does have a funny side. So if you can learn something useful and have a laugh along the way, I'll have done my job.

The book follows the best map a doctor has: the human body. Starting at the top and working down to the toes and fingers, delving inside to see what isn't apparent from the outside— the blood, the stomach, and the wonders of reproduction and the sex drive. We can't ignore the body's largest organ, the skin. Nor can we forget about the body as a whole, our preoccupation with fitness and our belief that we can conquer all illness.

Medicine, whether you think of it as an art or a science, is full of mysteries. But if this book succeeds in demystifying and de-mythifying a few far-fetched fancies, it'll be just as good for you as an apple a day.

Ted Boadway, MD
Toronto
June 1987

TAKING
it from the Top

Part I: The Outside

ALL THAT GLISTENS

People say that shiny hair is healthy hair. Of course we all know a few men who'd settle for any hair – shiny or otherwise – but we'll save that for later. For the moment, I'll try to ignore my receding hairline and shiny forehead.

The truth is that shiny hair is not necessarily healthy hair – it's really a matter of physics, not biology. It's a surface phenomenon revealing how much light the hair reflects, not its condition.

If a surface reflects light in an organized fashion, we see it as a shine. If it reflects light in a disorganized or scattered way, we perceive it as dullness. There are lots of people with perfectly healthy hair that doesn't reflect light well. The more curly your hair is, the less reflective it will be. Kinkiness may be interesting in other aspects of life, but, when it comes to hair, kinkiness is dull.

The "ideal" look of hair, if you are to go by the television commercials, is almost carved, not combed – a very smooth, reflective surface that literally shines back at you. Only statues and professional models can maintain that illusion.

The most important thing about healthy hair is that it's on your head and not in the bathtub. Hair itself, biologically speaking, is dead matter. Once hair is formed, it's neither more nor less healthy. It's hair, that's all.

What most of us consider "unhealthy" hair usually grows out of healthy hair follicles. It's just that the hair fibres aren't the best quality. But if you are suffering from a protein deficiency or calorie malnutrition, you can have unhealthy follicles that produce poor hair fibres. In our society the massive protein deficiency that would create unhealthy follicles is rare.

Hair *is* affected by certain vitamins. If your body lacks them, your hair production will definitely be "unhealthy." When I practised in West Africa, I saw some truly unhealthy scalps and unhealthy-looking hair. But this was a society in which malnutrition was a fact of life for many people, and there's no doubt that their deficiencies in protein, calories, and vitamins did affect the look of their hair. But this was the least of their problems.

In North America, where we have the luxury of worrying about the look of our hair, its appearance has more to do with the oiliness of our scalps than with the hair itself. All of us naturally produce different amounts of oil in our scalp. Some of us are capable of making two, three, and four times as much oil from our skin as others. And hair that is slightly oiled will better reflect light. If you get downright greasy, your hair will be very shiny indeed – but that's not very healthy for your hair or your scalp.

Shampoo contains detergent or soap to remove the natural oils. If you simply left it at that, your hair would probably feel dry and look dull. That's why shampoo also contains oil – you take out most of the old oil (and, you hope, the dirt) but replace it with new oil from the shampoo or a conditioner.

Now, if I were selling shampoos and various hair preparations, I would spread the myth that shiny hair is healthy hair. I would try to create an ideal that not many people can achieve, and then I'd tell them that my marvellous product will do it for them. When you see gorgeous men or women with carefully groomed hair (which most of us don't have) and you believe that they are somehow healthier than the rest of us because their hair is so shiny, you're going to want to buy the product that the models in the commercials are supposedly using.

The health angle has become extremely important in a lot of advertising. It's not enough for advertisers to say you're going to look good; it helps to imply that your general health will somehow be improved. There's a tremendous amount of talk of protein and amino acids in hair preparations. And most of it is, quite frankly, scientific poppycock.

If you read the product labels with an understanding of the science involved, you'll realize most of it is just puffery. Protein and vitamins in a shampoo might sound healthy (you know they are important for the look of the hair fibres), but the truth is they can be absorbed by the body only when you eat them. Pouring them on your head isn't going to make a hair of difference.

THE OLD GREY HAIR, IT AIN'T WHAT IT USED TO BE

If you've ever looked at yourself in the mirror in the morning and noticed a few more strands of silver than there were the night before, you might find yourself wondering what it was that shocked you so because, according to the myth, a great fright can turn your hair white overnight.

Now here's a real shocker: it isn't true.

First, let's look at how hair gets its colour. A hair is formed in a follicle – which is just an altered part of ordinary skin. And, like ordinary skin, it contains pigment-forming cells. Hair is just dead skin which, on any other part of our body, would simply become loose and shed. But on our head, and on select other areas, it grows, carrying the pigment for black, or blond, or chestnut with it.

Once the pigment is in there, it's in there – you can't get it out. The tip of my hair is as dead as it can be, and a long way away from my blood vessels. How can the pigment be "frightened" out of it? Well, it can't be.

So when hair does go grey, or white, or both, how does it happen? There is no simple answer. For some reason that we don't understand, the pigment cells stop making pigment. Although the hair continues to be formed, the cells are no longer packed with pigment, and the strands become almost colourless cells. They look white only because of the way light hits them.

Perhaps the myth developed after the fact. Middle age is one of the times of greatest stress– whether with family life and growing children, or with personal relationships and work. Middle age is also the time when hair starts to turn grey. So in our folklore we have connected two chance occurrences. However, this myth is ancient – it's found in old Christian and Jewish writings.

No one can predict or explain when grey hair will start, but one thing is sure: there's a strong genetic influence at play. If your parents' heads turned white early, take comfort that your behaviour as a child was not the cause of it. But chances are their parents' hair was also grey early. If you have a grandfather who went to his grave with a thick head of black hair, chances are you will too.

If you're a lucky man who keeps his locks bushy and brown, don't take it for granted that all the other parts of you will keep that youthful look. You might decide to grow a beard and discover, to your horror, it comes in full of more salt than pepper. Just as there is a difference in the texture of hair on various parts of our body, so there can be a difference in its natural colour. And don't be surprised if the buzz starts: "My goodness, hasn't John gone grey!"

Well, the rest of you hasn't changed, but that grey beard front and centre is hard to miss. In merely three weeks, you got old.

Three weeks, though, still aren't the same as overnight. We've all heard the story of the Second World War pilot who landed his fighter bomber in a field with three-quarters of his wings missing and the engine spluttering. When he emerged, his hair was pure white. The story must be apocryphal because I can't think of a single thing – other than having a bleach bomb go off in his helmet – that would cause such a dramatic change.

So how did we come to associate the sudden whiteness of hair with a sudden shock? Well, supposing you've just gone through a severe crisis and your whole physical demeanour has changed. People who saw you as a normal person with a spring in your step suddenly notice the outward signs of stress.And they'll notice – perhaps for the first time – all the grey on your head.

There is a hopeful note in all this gloomy grey: you can regain your natural colour faster than you lost it. There are some terrific hair dyes on the market and, if you don't feel right about the silver streaks, I heartily recommend them.

A BALD-FACED LIE

Before I get into this particular patch (or lack of it), I think it's only fair to describe my own condition. I do have a widow's peak, but I'm not what you would call bald. But then again, I might get more of a suntan than some people. The way my hairline is creeping up, I could take comfort in the myth that baldness is a sign of virility. It's a myth I wish everyone believed. Unfortunately, however, there isn't a convincing case to be made for the relationship between my masculinity and the quantity of my hair.

Though baldness is genetically programmed, the condition certainly occurs mostly in males. So there does seem to be some connection between higher androgen levels and the classic male pattern of baldness. Perhaps God made men bald because He gave women cellulite. It might be the divine balance of nature.

Obviously, men rather like the myth of virility and baldness. There are great benefits to be gained from continuing to lie about it. But since I do have a duty as a scientific person to tell the objective truth, I'll admit it's possible for a man with a full head of hair to be quite sexy.

Men didn't come up with this myth all on their own, though. I think women have probably played a supporting role in creating it. Women, being kind and often loving creatures, look for ways to prop their guy up. And what could be better than to tell him, "Dear, you must be more virile than the rest. I know you are." I think it is a happy collusion between the sexes.

And for the time being, it's the best cure we have. All the wonders of modern medical science haven't come up with anything to treat this particular male malaise. There have been nostrums propagated for centuries, but not one of them has proved effective.

But we keep hoping. In the medical literature there have been sporadic and encouraging reports. In fact, at the moment there are very cheering reports about a certain new cream that may have some beneficial effects. It's called Minoxidol, but I don't want to raise false hopes – or hairs. Even its proponents agree it only works for some people and then may produce fuzz rather than hair. Furthermore you must use it forever if you wish to maintain whatever you get.

In my opinion, you'd be better off with false hair than a false remedy. In that area, technology really has progressed. Years ago you could spot a rug from seventy-five paces. Nowadays you almost have to try to pull one off before you can be absolutely sure. And some of them you can't pull off if you try – they are surgically attached to the scalp by little latches.

And then there are transplants. A transplant takes a little punch-out of hair follicles from a spot where you don't usually lose hair or need it, such as the lower back of your head or around the rim, and repots the follicles where they'll do your ego some good.

Meanwhile, I still feel futile standing in front of a mirror in the morning watching myself shaving hair off my face while it's disappearing all by itself off the top of my head. Maybe it's time to invent a face-lift that lifts *all* the way up.

Part II: The Inside

WHY YOU GET A KICK FROM CHAMPAGNE

L et's celebrate your good health with a glass of champagne. One thing about the bubbly, however: it'll make you drunk pretty fast, faster than a speeding Singapore Sling – at least that's what a lot of people believe.

My theory about champagne is that it's usually drunk at midnight, at the end of a long evening; chances are there's been a lot of alcohol consumed beforehand. It's drunk to mark a special occasion – a wedding, birth, job promotion, whatever – something that has everyone high to begin with. So it's not surprising that people are somewhat intoxicated after they've drunk their champagne. But it is true, at least in theory, that it could make you a little bit drunker a little bit quicker than ordinary wine does.

It's the bubbles that do it. Alcohol is absorbed straight across the lining of our intestines and goes directly into the blood stream. When it hits the stomach lining, in it goes. The bubbles agitate the contents of the stomach and strip off the gastric juices that coat it, giving the alcohol more direct access to the lining. You might get the same effect from drinking a rye-and-ginger if the ginger ale has lots of fizz.

When we drink, we tend to feel intoxication when the alcohol level in the blood is on a rapid increase. You tend to down your first drink quickly; if your stomach is empty, the alcohol is absorbed right away, making you feel heady. By the second or third drink, even if you're consuming at the same rate, you don't get that drunken feeling because the alcohol level in your blood stream isn't shooting up. But the alcohol is impairing your perceptions all the same. It's the rate of increase of alcohol in your blood that makes you feel heady, more than the actual level.

There's a tremendous amount of mythology surrounding champagne. Some people believe that simply sniffing a champagne cork or inhaling the bubbles will lift them off the ground. But I'm sure that's just part of the mystique. All that comes off the bubbles is carbon dioxide. Carbon dioxide is about five per cent of what you breathe out on a regular basis. So chances are the little bit of carbon dioxide that comes out of champagne isn't going to do very much to you at all.

Champagne is accused of other villainies as well. People say it makes them sleepy, gives them a headache or a worse hangover than virtually anything else.

These things are true to the extent that they are true about all alcohol. But when people drink champagne they tend to drink lots of it and it often follows other types of alcohol. One bottle goes down so nicely and fast that you have to reach for the next. So if you fall asleep more quickly, your head pounds more painfully or your hangover is worse than with other kinds of booze, blame the quantity, not the quality, of what you've put down.

There are differences in the way drinks affect you. There is, for example, a real case to be made that red wine packs more of a punch than white. When juice ferments to wine, the process produces a host of chemicals, not the least of which is alcohol. The range of chemicals in red wine is more complex than in white. Esters, for example, give a red wine its nose. But like all chemicals, they interact with each person's body chemistry in a different way. So some people can drink a certain type of red wine, but not another, heavier type which contains more esters.

As for drinking champagne out of a slipper, I'd like to have a look at the slipper first. I know for a fact that drinking *anything* out of an old Oxford is bound to give you a headache.

THE MORNING AFTER THE NIGHT BEFORE

Lord knows there are endless cures for hangovers. Here are some of the ones you may have heard of and swear by: pop a Vitamin C before you start to drink; take an Aspirin before you go to bed; drink flat beer for breakfast. Even thinking about hangovers makes me a bit ill.

Anyone who has ever experienced a hangover knows what it's like. But for the few lucky souls who have never overdone a bit of liquid camaraderie, I'll try to explain what you've been missing.

These are the symptoms of a hangover: the first is an upset stomach, which can be quite mild or severe enough to make you vomit considerably. You might not even know it, but you could be bleeding from your stomach. The second is a terrible thirst. Then there's the classic headache, the one that's given rise to all those ice-pack-on-the-head images. And then – and quite surprising to most people – there's wakefulness. You turn in after a long and late night only to find yourself awake a few hours after you went to sleep. The one symptom everyone around you is bound to notice is jangling nerves and an excessive sensitivity to sound and light. It might make for a few cheap laughs in a sitcom, but for the sufferer it's very real.

You see, under the influence, your brain becomes hyperactive. Alcohol is a depressant. Your brain tries to keep its activity at a constant level. When you take a depressant, the control centre turns up the level of activity in an attempt to compensate. Then as you metabolize the alcohol, the control centre has to readjust. In the few hours it takes to get back to normal, you could feel like a basket case, with trembling hands and a hysterical reaction to a ringing doorbell.

Another thing alcohol affects is your urine flow. You might drink a two-ounce martini and find yourself a while later peeing out what seems like a bottleful. Letting out more than you take in might leave you profoundly dehydrated. You feel thirsty all the time because your whole body is desperate for liquid. This is the reason, believe it or not, you have the headache: your brain actually shrinks in its cavity and the vessels get stretched until you feel like a pinhead. If you joggle your head a little bit, the vessels stretch more – so you wind up walking as though on eggs.

The secret is to drink – but not more booze, I beg you. I have a hard time understanding the "hair of the dog" remedy (drinking more of what got you into this mess in the first place). Quaffing something non-alcoholic before you hit the potent potables, or mixing the hard stuff with soft as you go isn't going to solve the problem. You're going to pee it all away while under the influence. So when you're finished drinking, before you go to bed, and certainly every time you get up in the night, down a soft drink or a glass of water. You've lost a lot of sodium and potassium salts in the urine you've been passing. Fruit juices are especially helpful because they contain these natural salts.

If you refuse to relinquish the "hair of the dog" myth, stick to beer. At least there's fluid in a bottle of beer, and the bit of alcohol that's in it will calm your activating system for a while. But it really just prolongs the problem. If you are at the point where this is your accepted cure, the chances are astronomical that you are a problem drinker (and, true to the condition, you will deny it). Once you dry out, it's time to go for professional help.

Some people swear by a glass of milk to "coat their stomach." It does help. Alcohol is a direct stomach irritant and it stimulates acid secretion. So if you drink milk before hitting the sauce, it will have a neutralizing, buffering effect. And if you drink it afterwards, it will neutralize the excess acid production. But remember: the inflammation caused by the excess acid and the direct irritation of the stomach by alcohol can lead to a full-blown gastric hemorrhage. Milk isn't strong enough to prevent what could become a profound medical emergency.

That's also why the Aspirin remedy is a myth worth debunking. People take three Aspirin before they go to bed and they forget that Aspirin is a tremendous gastric irritant. Combine it with excessive alcohol intake and you're just looking for trouble.

Vitamin C is an acid too but it's very weak. Compared to hydrochloric acid, which your stomach makes, it's quite mild. I'm not convinced it does any good, but at least it can't do you any harm.

Among remedies I've heard touted, the most radical is the "Prairie Oyster." You make it by putting a raw egg and some Worcestershire sauce in a toothbrush glass, stirring the contents with a toothbrush and swallowing the whole mess. I can't see any medical logic behind this one, but I do recommend you keep a toilet bowl handy when you try it.

The only real treatment for a hangover is prevention. I'm not asking you to join the Temperance Union. I'm just trying to warn you that some good times can hurt an awful lot the next day.

IT'S A KNOCKOUT

There's Our Hero, up on the movie screen. The Bad Guy hits him over the head with a chair. Our Hero crumples to the floor. When he gets up he shakes his head. He might have a bit of a headache, but he's none the worse for wear. With a one-two, he knocks out the Bad Guy. And rides off into the sunset.

Nice script. But what happens in real life, as opposed to reel life, when you get crunched on the noggin? You'd be damn lucky to get up and walk away, movie style. You would probably have a concussion. And it might be serious.

"Concussion" isn't used very much any more as a medical term, but it is descriptive. A concussion is the result of a "concussive force," a shock wave that goes through your brain matter and everything else that's in your head. A blow to the head can start the wave moving.

If the blow is strong enough to render you unconscious, chances are that you have been dealt a very significant, lasting injury. You may be one of those fortunate few who spring up ready to fight again. But lesser mortals run the risk of short-term or even long-term impaired mental function.

The brain is a relatively gelatinous thing sitting inside a hard box, the skull. When the box is hit, it could break, causing a fracture. But even if it doesn't, the force sends shock waves travelling across the brain. And shock waves can be powerful enough to cause shearing injuries.

A shock wave passing through the brain can even make the liquid in it boil – if just for a millisecond. But this is very serious because the bubbles of the boiling fluids can cause tremendous disruption in the tissue.

There are two ways in which something can be said to "boil." The first (the one we're most familiar with) is as a result of heat energy. The second is the effect of pressure with which molecules are held together. The force of a concussion momentarily reduces the pressure binding the molecules, so they jump apart and become a vapour. That's boiling. As soon as that shock wave passes, the pressure rises again, pushing the molecules back together. That's called "condensing." It all happens very rapidly, but a millisecond is all it takes for the damage to be done.

A more familiar example might be what happens to astronauts up in space. If they didn't have their suits on to keep the pressure inside, their blood would boil because of the lack of pressure, not because they are overheated. It's exactly the same kind of phenomenon. And it isn't good.

Obviously, if you're knocked unconscious, there's not an awful lot you can do to help yourself. But what should you do if you're around when Our Hero is knocked down?

The best thing is to leave him alone. But before you do, make sure his airway isn't obstructed in any way. Most people recover from head injuries, but if they can't breathe within three minutes, they're not going to recover from anything.

So if Our Hero has slumped forward, you should raise his head gently to let him get all the oxygen he needs. If he has fallen face down into a puddle of whisky or water, move him out of it because as little as three centimetres of liquid is enough to drown a man who's unconscious. Prop up any dangling parts, like arms or legs, that might get twisted and hurt in the twenty minutes or so it will take him to return to the world of the living. Then go find some professional help.

Don't try to revive Our Hero. In reel life, someone might pour a bucket of cold water on his head. It's not going to wake him up any faster and it might make him angry. And those brisk little slaps on the face are worth trying only if you have some sort of a vengeance against him.

Otherwise, they'll just serve to annoy him.

Spirits of ammonia, or smelling salts, are supposed to revive people too. Have you ever tried them when you're awake? It's like a quick trip to the dry cleaner's or emptying out the kitty litter. I wouldn't do it to anybody you know, awake or unconscious. When you see a fight trainer waft something under the nose of a groggy boxer, it's really a kind of psychotherapy to snap his brain to attention. It won't do a thing for someone who's out cold.

Being knocked out is certainly not a healthy thing, but it does have a sort of fun side. Remember all those comic strip characters flat on their backs with stars and planets revolving around their heads? Well, the light show inside your head really does happen.

It's visual evidence of the shock wave going through your brain. The occipital lobe, the back part of your brain just about at the bottom of your hairline, is where you decode the electrical messages coming from your eye. When a concussive wave passes through the brain, it's capable of causing an electrical discharge in the cells of the occiput. You see it as light. It's a disorganized light which you'll register as little bunches that look like stars, or as a broad band that looks like a multi-coloured flash. It's real, all right.

A rock concert will give you the same effect. And, despite what parents say, cause less brain damage.

WHAT THE NOSE KNOWS

Nosebleeds do not look nice, but usually they look worse than they are. Of course, if the air is dry or you live at a high altitude, chances are you're going to get nosebleeds more easily. At least that's the conventional wisdom we're going to put to the test.

For once, the conventional wisdom is right. Dry air indeed is the biggest culprit, and high altitude doesn't help either. (Nosebleeds resulting from an injury are a whole different ballgame and one that we're not playing here.)

First we need to understand why the nose is more prone to bleeding than other areas of the body. In the septum of your nose – the central part that runs right from the front of your nose clear through to the back and separates the two halves – you have a tremendous concentration of blood vessels called a "plexus." It performs an important function: large volumes of air pass though the nasal cavities on both sides of the septum, and if it didn't have a capacity to distribute a lot of warm, wet blood, the nose would freeze and/or dry out.

In order for this ingenious system to work, the blood vessels have to be very close to the surface and thin-walled so that the transfer is rapid. Now, if you have thin-walled vessels with a high blood flow under some pressure, it's not surprising that once in a while one of them lets loose.

The air going into your lungs must be completely moist or your lungs would dry out – something your body can't afford. So if the air you are breathing is dry, it's up to your nose to moisten it before it enters your lungs. As a result, the moisture is taken up from the membranes in your nose and they dry out.

Normally, you make a couple of jugfuls of mucus in your nose each day. You don't even notice when you swallow it and it's re-absorbed through your stomach. But if some of this mucus dries out because of the intense dryness of the environment, it can form small crusts that sit on top of the blood vessels in your septum. If the crusts break, their sharp edges may lacerate this very fragile vessel, and there you go: a nosebleed.

As you go up in altitude, the external pressure drops, but inside your head the pressure stays as before. This creates an imbalance. If you have one blood vessel that's especially fragile and close to breaking, this difference between external and internal pressure is all it needs to rupture and bleed.

The resulting mess can be quite scary. All that blood in the middle of your face makes you look like a rerun of M*A*S*H. So the first and most important thing to do when a nosebleed starts up is to sit down and be quiet. The worst thing that you can do is become excited and get your blood pressure up and your pulse racing. And this is even more important if the nosebleed isn't on your face but on your child's. A parent must let the child know, "This is something we can handle." If you can't project calmness, how can you expect a kid not to become agitated?

Someone with a nosebleed, no matter what age, should remain sitting up. If you lie down, your veins fill and put more pressure on the system. So sit up, calm down. Then grab hold of your nose. Between your eyes you'll feel a hard bony part in your nose at the smallest point. Follow it down until your fingers fall off the bone – there, at the fleshy part, you've hit the plexus.

Now hold it shut. The whole thing, not just the tip. To stop the bleeding, you have to hold the plexus shut for *ten to fifteen minutes*. That's a long time. You wouldn't believe how long ten minutes is when you're holding your nose. And you can't switch hands or let go to see if the bleeding has stopped because then you have to start timing all over again.

You may have seen movies in which the heroine, a delicate little flower, puts an ice pack across the top of her nose or across the bridge. But for that to work, she'd have to apply enough cold for long enough to freeze her nose solid between her eyes and her lips. For Scarlett O'Hara, tomorrow might be another day, but where is she going to find another nose?

Another popular remedy that has a bit more to recommend it is to blow your nose with some force to get as much blood as possible out at once. Be warned that you'll have lots of loose blood in the nasal cavity and it will form somewhat alarming-looking clots. But it's important to empty them out so that you don't have a massive obstruction in your nose.

However it's only a part solution. The tear in your blood vessels is actually trying to heal itself – the reason clots are forming around it. Tiny fragments of cells called "platelets" are building up alongside the tear. They form like grains of sand in the blood flow to create an initial plug. The first plug stays in place just long enough to give off natural chemicals that will form a permanent block.

Now, if during that time you blow your nose, you'll whoosh away the platelet aggregates that have built up. And your nose is back to square one. The platelets have to start building a clot all over again. So blow your nose to get rid of the first clot and see if the bleeding has stopped. If you still have a clot in your nose after that, leave it there. Nature's own process will dissolve it in a couple of hours and it will just drain away.

A nosebleed in a normal healthy adult is not uncommon and certainly not a cause for alarm. The elderly, however, can experience nosebleeds that aren't from the plexus but from arterial sources much farther back in the nose. That sort of nosebleed can be very profound, can even be life-threatening and requires rather dramatic methods. But fortunately, it happens very rarely.

What panics most people is that their kids always seem to get nosebleeds. It is true that the phenomenon is much more common among the "Sesame Street" set. Children have smaller nasal passages than we do, so these are more prone to crusting. They also tend to be restless sleepers, and if they are constantly turning over and rubbing their nose across the pillow, sooner or later they'll break a little crust loose and it will lacerate a vessel.

Of course, two tablespoons of blood on their pillow isn't very much, but it looks like a slaughterhouse. They'll wander into your room in the middle of the night, crying their hearts out, looking as if they've been in a fist fight, and every alarm in your head and your heart goes off. That's when you *really* need to remain calm.

ACHOO, ACHOO, ACHOO

The number of myths surrounding the simple act of sneezing is mind-blowing. I've heard that some people sneeze in twos and threes, never just once. I've heard that your heart stops momentarily when you sneeze. And I've also heard that you can hurt yourself if you stifle a sneeze.

It is true that some people tend to have fixed sneezing patterns. I, for example, am a two-time sneezer. If I sneeze once, I will certainly sneeze again. But I will rarely sneeze three times.

Unfortunately, some people, once they start sneezing, can hardly stop. I know a woman who counted thirty-nine sneezes in a row. She says she almost died, which is unlikely, but it certainly was distressing.

We don't know why people sneeze in patterns. But we do know why people sneeze. Sneezing has a function: it clears materials from the nasal passage. When we cough, we're clearing material from our lower respiratory tract, just below the vocal chords and in the windpipe. With a sneeze, we close our soft palate at the back, building up pressure because our lips and tongue are also closed. Then the soft palate releases and the air explodes with great velocity. When you have an irritation in the nose, sneezing is a good way to get rid of it.

Sometimes, however, it's an irritation you can't clear – hay fever, for example. The nose is extremely irritated because pollens have settled in it and caused inflammation. However it won't blow away. But how does one explain the sunlight sneezers? As soon as they go outdoors when the sun is shining, AAAAAA-Choooooooo. Are they allergic to the sun? Nor do I understand people who sneeze when they eat oranges–something about citric acid seems to do it for them.

As for your heart stopping, yes, indeed it does. Sort of. When you sneeze, your chest muscles contract quite strongly and you build up pressure in your thoracic cavity. You actually close off the exit vessels from your heart, the aorta. There you have sensors that control a natural pacemaker mechanism. When you alter the pressure in your chest, it can actually alter the rhythm of your heart. The process may be preceded by a temporary slowdown and then a catch-up phase. Most of us wouldn't even be aware of it. It doesn't "stop" in a life-threatening sense, but it is a momentary pause before starting up a new pace.

When you stifle a sneeze, it's not what you do that can hurt you, but what you don't do. You don't release the pressure. I once saw a man reaching over the back of his car seat to adjust his child's seat belt before they drove off. Just at that point, he needed to sneeze. He stifled it so that he wouldn't sneeze on his child. But because of the angle he was at and the tremendous pressure, he actually cracked a rib. He may have been a heroic father, but all he got for his pains was, well, pain.

There are a few unfortunate people who can hurt themselves by sneezing because their Eustachian tubes, the tubes to the middle ear, are "patent" or open most of the time. The majority of us keep our Eustachian tubes closed and open them up only when we swallow or yawn. We know they open because we often hear a *pop!*

Someone with constantly patent Eustachian tubes might build up enough pressure with a sneeze to actually blow the eardrum. The same thing could happen to a person who has a fragile eardrum perforated by multiple childhood ear infections. It doesn't happen very often, but it does happen.

If your ears aren't fragile and you're not sitting in a wrenched-up position when you feel a sneeze coming on, let it come. But if once you start sneezing you just can't quit, there are cures. They all work by interrupting the tickling sensation in the reflex at the back of your nose. One of the most effective things you can do is snuffle some tap water up your nose. Tap water is sterile, so it won't do any damage. It sounds weird but it really works.

Or try eating a soda cracker. It's dry and feels like sand in the back of your throat. That causes a counter-irritation and makes you forget the irritation in your nose. Sneezing doesn't do much for me – I have to find my kicks in other parts of the body. But apparently people have thought of it as fun. Why else would snuff have been invented?

DON'T CUT IT OUT!

When I was a kid back in the Bronze Age, getting your tonsils out was as common as getting the measles. After all, a person doesn't *need* tonsils, right? You might as well get them out of the way whether they are infected or not. That was the prevailing wisdom back in those dark days and it prevailed upon me and practically every other kid I knew.

Fortunately, things have changed. We're much more conservative about surgery these days. For tonsils to go, they must be really bad.

Before we talk about their bad condition, we should talk about what tonsils do. Individually they don't pay their way in the body, but collectively they do. They belong to a great collective called the lymphoid system and they themselves are really just a specific collection of lymph nodes, one on either side of the throat. The main job of the lymph nodes is to recognize foreign invaders and fight them off. So, they have a protective role, rather like the DEW line. This particular ring is important in immune fighting, but the tonsil bits are not that critical.

Only one other part of the ring has a particular name: the adenoids. The others are unsung warriors in the fight against disease. The adenoids used to be removed at the same time as the tonsils: one-stop shopping in the operating room and "the works" were gone.

Nowadays, your tonsils are removed only when they become badly and chronically infected. Tonsils have deep pits, visible only as little openings. These pits sometimes harbour bacteria and just when you get over one infection, bingo! you're on to another.

These repetitious infections can really disable you. You ask yourself which is better: putting up with chronic recurrent infections or having your tonsils removed? The deciding factor is often knowing that they are quite destroyed anyway. Obviously your body has learned to get along without that particular lymphatic tissue by now. It has been so damaged that you aren't removing anything that matters functionally any more.

Fortunately, progress on other fronts has made the tonsillectomy less necessary. Antibiotics can now clear up severe infections with alacrity. Recent research has helped determine more precisely when a tonsillectomy will make a difference in a patient's overall health.

If you have been living "tonsil-free" the last few years, there's no need to worry about it. If your tonsils were the cause of chronic infections, obviously you are better off without them. You can get throat infections for all sorts of reasons and you are no more prone to them *sans* tonsils than a person who still has the little flappers. You also don't really have to worry about being less immune than anyone else – you have a tremendous amount of lymphatic tissue elsewhere in your body which is quite capable of recognizing invaders and mounting a defence through your immune system. You needn't consider yourself a member of a particularly disadvantaged majority.

About the only thing that has been lost in the trend toward fewer tonsillectomies is the chance for a kid to pig out on ice cream. Those of you who had your tonsils out as kids may remember your parents trying to comfort you in the face of the operation by promising you all the ice cream you could eat. Well, there was a scientific reason for that promise; it wasn't merely a kindness and a consolation. In a post-surgery state, you have higher caloric requirements than normal. You have to eat something and, since you're probably feeling weak and fragile, that something might as well be comfortable going down your throat.

Ice cream is ideal. It's cold and slippery and has loads of calories. Jell-o is good, too, but it's not as rich. Popsicles aren't half-bad, either.

So if you're one of those people who grew up in the Fifties and had your tonsils out because it was The Thing To Do, don't feel robbed by the fact that medical attitudes have changed. You got the ice cream and your kid probably won't.

SIGHT
for Sore Eyes

WHEN THE LIGHTS ARE LOW

C hildhood has a lot more than ten commandments. "Thou shalt not read under the covers with a flashlight" is one we all remember. Parents, of course, do not want their youngsters staying up late, but they're also concerned that reading with very little light is going to damage their children's eyes.

Getting the kids to sleep at a decent hour is still a legitimate concern and enough reason to keep this particular commandment in force. But the fear of damaging the eyes doesn't hold up in the light of day.

The myth probably had its beginnings in the days when people read by candlelight – until electricity was invented, they had no other choice. Except, perhaps, to go to bed. In any case, as their vision got poorer (as it usually does, even today, with advancing age), they wanted to ascribe it to something. So they blamed the innocent candlelight.

The truth of the matter is that reading in low light really isn't hard on your eyes at all. Seeing is a chemical reaction. When light falls upon the retina, certain natural chemicals are broken down. This breakdown releases energy that's converted to electrical energy. It passes through the nerves into the brain and *voilà*, you have vision! When you read in low light, it simply means you don't break down as much of the chemical as you do with floodlights glaring. The signal your brain receives is lower, and so it seems it is more difficult to read. But the process doesn't do any damage.

31

"Aha!" you say. "Even if your eyes keep working fine, surely you'll get eyestrain!" Sorry. You can't get eyestrain from a chemical reaction, and it's chemistry we're talking about.

Eyestrain is commonly caused by muscle imbalance, which occurs when you have to work the muscles of your eyes harder to make you see. This happens to people who are short- or long-sighted who keep their eyes busy for long periods of time without help from corrective lenses. The little muscles in their eyes actually do have to work harder and might feel tired or sore after eight hours of going over legal briefs. The sufferers call it "eyestrain." But there's no proof that reading in low light exacerbates the symptoms.

The eyes are a marvellous example of clever engineering, built to withstand all sorts of changes. But they work at their own speed and with their own logic. Take, for example, the process of adjusting to really bright light when you come out of a dark room, or vice versa.

When you've been in darkness for a while, the natural chemicals in the eye build up to a very high level because they're not being broken down. When you step out into the light, things look washed out at first and you have to squint. That's because your eyes are on overload. You have more chemicals in your eyes than you need and they're sending too many signals to your brain. But gradually the chemical level in the retina is knocked down to a new homeostasis, or balance.

When you go back into the darkness, you need those chemicals to build up again. It takes fifteen to twenty minutes for your body to regenerate the proper level. If you think that's too long, speak to your clergyman and ask him to put in a word.

TV OR NOT TV?

You do know, of course, that television is bad for your health. I'm not talking about mind rot from "Love Boat" reruns. I'm talking about sitting too close to the television set. It ruins your eyes. At least that's what many parents claim.

Let's zoom in for a close-up on this myth. No matter where you are sitting, whether it's on a comfortable chair at a good distance or with your nose pressed up against the screen, your eyes are capable of adjusting quite well to the brightness of the TV set. The intensity of TV light is nothing compared to being outside on a sunny day. And the muscles that work your eyes can accommodate the close vision without any risk of damage.

This myth is an example of symptoms being mistaken for the

cause. Little Johnny sits right up against the set. Dad says, "Johnny, why don't you sit farther back?" Johnny doesn't want to, and a little running tiff inevitably follows.

One day, Dad decides to take Johnny to have his eyes checked. And, lo and behold! Johnny is short-sighted. And he needs to wear glasses. So Dad says, "You see? I told you if you sat too close to the television that your eyes would be ruined."

In fact, it was the other way around. Johnny gradually moved closer and closer to the screen as his eyes deteriorated to the point that he *needed* to be that close to see it well. Children themselves are rarely aware that their vision is poor.

Dad may have lost this round, but he's not out yet. TV screens leak radiation, right? Parents believe, logically enough, that the closer you are to the source of radiation, the more dangerous it is.

Radiation is an important issue, but as far as TV sets are concerned, we can stop worrying. The same goes for video display terminals, which are basically just another type of TV set. No one sits closer to a tube than a VDT operator – much closer than you'd ever watch television. In fact, VDTs are made smaller than TV sets specifically to accommodate viewing at close range.

There has been, needless to say, a lot of research done on the issue of radiation and TV because this is a very real worry. The very word "radiation" has a bad reputation and mostly (witness Chernobyl) for good reason. But people forget there are different types of radiation and not all of it is harmful.

Light is a form of radiation. It contains both infrared radiation and ultraviolet radiation. Infrared is simply heat energy – and sitting in front of a cozy fire isn't going to hurt you. Ultraviolet radiation is carried by sunlight and can be damaging if your skin is over-exposed to it for long periods of time.

The really bad stuff is ionizing radiation. We most often come into contact with it as x-rays which can damage our molecular structure. Microwave radiation, too, can be harmful in large amounts.

Television sets and video display terminals don't give off any ionizing radiation. Nor do they emit microwaves. The circuitry just isn't capable of producing those kinds of radiation. And there is less ultraviolet and infrared radiation given off than you'd be exposed to outdoors. Radiation frequencies are measurable very close to the screen, but at the distance an operator or viewer is sitting they are negligible.

It is true that at certain companies and in certain cities, pregnant women wear lead aprons when operating video display terminals. I think this is an over-reaction. There was some concern before proper research was done on the exact amount of radiation being emitted. The lead apron thing started before all the facts were in. It's really unwarranted, but if it makes a pregnant woman feel protected, there's nothing wrong with it.

I can't guarantee that in thirty years something else won't come up that we didn't know about, so I am taking a chance by going on record with this opinion. But I do know we now have very sensitive methods of measuring ionizing radiation at extremely low levels. If you park a VDT between a couple of sensors and leave it there for days, they'll register nothing at all. I'm convinced that as far as ionizing radiation goes, the answer is in. There is no danger.

A darkened room lit only by the eerie blue glow of a TV set can look menacing. But we watch movies in dark rooms. In fact, if the movie theatre isn't dark, we complain. Television can't hurt us any more than looking directly at the moon on a pitch-black night. But with the moon you never feel the need to change the channel.

WHO'S THAT BEHIND THE SUNGLASSES?

The cool look wouldn't be complete without a pair of slick shades. You might be totally in fashion, but will wearing sunglasses damage your eyes? Some people believe sunglasses will make your eyes "lazy." At least that's what I hear parents tell their small children who want to get a pair of sunglasses.

Devious parents! I imagine kids would fall for that myth – in fact, it's usually the kids, not the parents, who ask me if it's true. But anyone whose age is in double digits has no reason to be fooled by it.

The tale sounds believable because everyone knows that after you take your sunglasses off on a sunny day, your eyes have trouble adjusting to the light. It may take up to five or six or seven minutes before you finally feel comfortable. It's easy to deduce that there's something wrong with your eyes. If they are "lazy," perhaps if you worked them more they would accommodate this brilliant light more quickly.

But wearing sunglasses doesn't mean your eyes aren't working hard. The problem is a matter of balance. When your eyes aren't exposed to much light, your pupils open up, the muscles relax and the natural chemicals in your retina get a chance to build up. When the light suddenly floods in, the chemicals start to break down, but there's so much of them, the reaction is extreme. Your pupils tighten down very hard, making you want to squint.

The muscles in your eyes, however, aren't bothered by this at all. They're constantly at work regardless of how much light is shining on them. They really don't need additional "exercise." They are not like skeletal muscles. They can't be developed the way your biceps and triceps can. Your eye muscles work out virtually twenty-four hours a day, even when you are dreaming. They don't have to "keep fit" – they do it by themselves all the time.

So wearing shades doesn't cause problems. But can *not* wearing them hurt you? Yes, but only in extreme situations. To avoid snow blindness, for one. Snow blindness commonly occurs in books that we read as kids about travelling the Arctic. Fortunately, in real life it is very rare. Proper sunglasses do prevent snow blindness and are a must when you explore the Pole. But in your normal, everyday adventures, you won't damage your eyes without them.

The darkness of the lenses, or their tint or colour doesn't make any difference. I personally like to see the world through rose-coloured glasses. It cheers me up, but it doesn't affect my eyesight one way or the other.

The "highway patrol" look does more than intimidate people. In fact, mirrored sunglasses are very good because they reflect a high percentage of light. I'm not too crazy about the "American Gigolo" variety of glasses that look like venetian blinds, with no lenses in them, only closely-louvred striations of plastic. But they are not necessarily harmful. If the effect is to reduce the percentage of the ambient light which reaches your eye, that's fine.

There is no such thing as "recommended" sunglasses. Some types of sunglasses are better suited to certain activities. For example, polarized glasses are very good for boaters because they cut down on the light from a horizontal reflective surface, the water. Some people like the kind of lenses which darken as the light gets brighter and fade when it fades. I like them because they are adaptable throughout the day.

Some people prefer darker lenses; some like them almost clear. As long as the lenses aren't scratched and are of reasonable quality, they won't distort your vision. It's simply a matter of personal taste – or whatever's raging in the fashion pages.

SEEING THROUGH CARROTS

There probably isn't a kid in the world whose mother didn't say, "Carrots are good for your eyes." So how come, after all those carrots, raw and snappy or cooked and mushy, we don't all have x-ray vision like Superman? The time has come to put that particular home-spun wisdom to the crunch.

Carrots, I'm sorry to say, *aren't* especially good for the eyesight – no more than any other food. But when I was a kid, I too believed they were, because that's what my mother told me. The Great Carrot Conspiracy was not, however, created spontaneously by moms just to get their kids to eat their vegetables. It was a conspiracy all right, a conspiracy for a very good cause: winning World War II.

There is a scientific germ of truth that connects carrots to the way the eyes work. The chemical that gives you good night vision – or any vision at all for that matter – is very similar to a natural chemical which occurs in carrots and gives them their colour: carotene. But that wasn't the source of the myth; it was the germ of scientific truth that made the myth more plausible.

Here's what happened: during the war years, psychologists discovered that if you used red lights rather than green lights on your dashboard, you broke down less of the chemical which naturally regenerates constantly in your eye and therefore your vision was better. This proved to be a very important discovery for airmen who flew at night. If they could see an enemy flyer before he saw them, they would have the jump on him and get the advantage in a dogfight.

So the Allies started to equip the dashboards of their planes with red lights. But they knew that the Germans would sooner or later realize something was amiss. They would start to wonder why the Allied pilots always saw their man first, and they would search through downed Allied wrecks more carefully to discover the secret or, worse, interrogate pilots they had taken as prisoners.

To take the focus off the red lights, the Royal Air Force decided to indulge in a subterfuge. They told their own pilots about the connection between the chemical in carrots and the chemical in the eye that regulates night vision. It sounded scientific and proper, so the pilots believed the story – which was exactly what the RAF wanted.

The airmen soon began to drink carrot juice, eat carrots for breakfast, carrots for lunch, carrots for supper until they were sick of carrots. But they *had* to eat them – they had been ordered to.

Furthermore, they were told this bizarre regimen was Top Secret; that if captured, they must tell no one. But the RAF knew that if one of their pilots fell into German hands and was interrogated about his "superior" vision, he would probably "confess" that it was all due to the carrots.

Of course, people can't keep secrets forever, especially under duress. Before long, everyone on the other side was eating carrots too. It was supposed to be a war secret, but at the end of the war it all came out. When the airmen returned home, they told their families and everyone else that "carrots are good for your eyes." My parents believed it, and I grew up believing it.

Later, of course, I learned the true dietary explanation for good eyesight. Vitamin A is critical for the eyesight and, if you had a Vitamin A deficiency, then any food which contains it (including carrots) would create a dramatic improvement. But if you have a normal, rounded North American diet, increasing the amount of any one thing you eat isn't going to sharpen your vision.

You can hurt your eyes by not eating properly, it's true. But to do that, you would have to have a massive general restriction of your dietary intake rather than a selective restriction. People on a hunger strike, for example, do become blind towards the terminal stages of their strike, but they are also almost dead at that point. It's not just their eyes that go from the malnutrition but various other vital functions as well.

Carrots *are* good for your eyes in the sense that they are good for all the rest of you too. Along with milk, bread, oranges, fish, cheese, broccoli ....

CHAPTER THREE

LIFE
and Breath

PIPE DOWN

Smoking is bad for you. That's an undebatable medical fact, and the only people who haven't heard the news yet have probably just returned from outer space. As a doctor and non-smoker, I can find nothing good to say about the habit. But there is a bit of folk wisdom that puts me between a rock and a hard place. And that is the idea that smoking a pipe is less harmful than smoking cigarettes.

As much as I loathe telling the truth on this particular issue, I have to admit that this myth has some facts behind it. I'm so opposed to smoking that to say anything positive about it really gives me extreme pain. In the interests of science and intellectual scrupulousness, however, I have to state that smoking a pipe is sometimes less harmful than smoking cigarettes.

It all depends on which diseases you're talking about. It's true that there is less chance of your dying from pipe smoking than from cigarette smoking. But pipe smoking carries its own risks, the biggest one being cancer of the lip. Cancer of the lip tends to be a treatable disease: it is right up front; it's easily seen; it can be chopped right out surgically; the cure rate is very high. About eighty per cent of the time it is not terminal. It looks funny and makes it difficult for you to pronounce certain words. But you survive.

Cigarette smoking, on the other hand, generates the considerably greater risks of lung cancer and heart disease, for which the mortality rates are abysmal. Pipe smokers don't contract these diseases to the extent that cigarette smokers do.

It is assumed pipe smokers don't inhale, but that's not exactly true. There have been excellent studies on inhalation which lead to the interesting conclusion that there are as many ways to smoke a pipe as there are shapes of pipe bowls.

There is the purist – a pipe smoker who has never smoked anything but the pipe. He (and it is invariably a he) rarely inhales. He therefore doesn't run the risk of lower airway diseases and the systemic effect throughout the body. Then there are the ex-cigarette smokers who have converted to the pipe. Many of these will inhale just as much as they did when they smoked cigarettes, but some convert to a purist smoking habit – they stop inhaling and, over a period of time, their risks of contracting inhalation diseases decline. Then there are the combination smokers who smoke cigarettes but light up a pipe from time to time to "cut down." Rubbish! They don't cut down. In fact, they inhale just as much as they do with cigarettes and deceive only themselves.

None of these types of pipe smokers takes into account the fact of second-hand smoke. The risks from second-hand smoke from any smoking materials – pipes or cigarettes – are about the same. Purist pipe smokers get into trouble because they are heavy second-hand smokers. Even though they don't inhale directly, their lower airways are still at risk because they envelop themselves with a cloud of smoke.

Second-hand pipe smoke is as much a problem for non-smokers as second-hand cigarette smoke. Even though many of us don't mind the smell of a pipe, we shouldn't be charmed by that woodsy aroma.

Nowadays we can measure nicotine levels in the blood very accurately. Several interesting things have come out in studies. First of all, when a smoker changes his smoking habits (especially if he becomes a combination smoker) he will almost invariably inhale enough pipe smoke to keep his nicotine levels exactly where they were when he smoked only cigarettes. A smoker, you see, sets a pattern for his level of addiction to nicotine. If he switches to lower nicotine and tar brands, he either smokes more of them or he smokes more of each individual cigarette to keep his levels right up there.

A pipe may be less addictive than a cigarette, but once the need for nicotine is established, it doesn't matter what is smoked. Smoking creates two kinds of addiction. One is the chemical addiction to nicotine and other substances. The other is a psychological addiction – the "I'm doing something with my mouth and hands routine" for which some pipe smokers are notorious. They can hardly ever get their pipe lit they are so busy doing something with it. Medically, a psychological addiction is easier to deal with than a true chemical addiction. You could conceivably persuade a pipe smoker that he should move on to worry beads. But a true addict needs the *chemical* fix. While many purist pipe smokers are merely psychologically addicted, most cigarette and combination smokers are truly addicted. So it is nonsense to argue that switching to a pipe is a way to wean yourself.

Still, as a doctor I would encourage a cigarette smoker to make the switch to a pipe in the hope that he will join that fifty or sixty per cent of converts who eventually become non-inhalers. He should realize that, once he starts smoking a pipe, the next thing he knows these little leather patches will start appearing at the elbows of his jacket and half-glasses will sprout at the end of his nose. It really is a frightening phenomenon.

BABY, IT'S COLD OUTSIDE

Don't go outside with your hair wet! You'll catch a cold. Don't stand in a draught! You'll catch a cold. Bundle up, it's cold outside! Wear your hat or you'll get an earache!" It all sounds perfectly logical, right? There seems to be an obvious connection between cold air and coming down with a chill. In movies people start sneezing almost as soon as they are out in the rain.

There is the obvious word association: we talk about *being* cold and *having* a cold. When you have a cold, you experience a lot of things associated with being cold. You might shiver, you feel cold as you're shivering, and you also feel as miserable having a cold as being out in the cold. But if it were true that being cold gives you a cold, then skiers would never be able to ski and outdoor workers in the winter would not be able to function. Nor, for that matter, would anyone having to leave a toasty house and wait for the car to warm up ever make it all the way to the office.

The illness that we call "a cold" is caused by viruses. There are fifty or more distinct viruses capable of giving us a cold regardless of the temperature outside. There is such a variety of viruses out there that we can't build up immunity to all of them. Therefore we can get a cold from one virus this week, and two weeks later we can get a cold from another virus. Even worse, we don't have an infinite immune memory for cold viruses – so we can catch a recycled cold, the same one we had two years ago. We're not "run down" and our immunity isn't "low." It's just bad luck.

Another myth about catching a cold is that the viruses are airborne. We have a mental picture of an explosive cough or sneeze creating a great hanging cloud of particles containing deadly viruses. You'd think a cough was radioactive.

The most common method of transmitting a virus, in fact, is person to person, hand to hand, hand to nose. It happens when people shake hands or pick up something touched by someone with a cold. The virus stays alive for a while on a coffee cup, say, or a pencil. We pick it up and touch our nose or rub our eyes – and the virus makes its way into our system.

There is also a myth about the time during which you can pass on a cold. You are contagious for several days before you know you have a cold. You might have picked up a virus a week ago, but today is the first day you feel unwell. So, unwittingly, you have run the risk of infecting others for the last three or four days. You'll stay contagious for another couple of days but decreasingly so. Once your cold has blossomed into the "code in the node," you aren't very contagious at all.

By the time you decide to stay home from work, you have already done in everyone in the office. If you feel miserable, by all means skip a day of work and stay in bed. But don't use the excuse that you are "thinking of the others." They're all home, too – thinking of you.

WHY YOUR KID IS A SNUFFLEUPAGUS

If a drippy nose seems to be a permanent fixture on your child's face, don't despair. Everybody knows that kids' noses run more than those of adults. It's a myth I can't debunk.

Adults have an experienced immune system and kids don't. When a child is born, her immune system is competent enough to recognize foreign invaders, but it's untried. By the time that child grows into an adult, her immune system will have run across an awful lot of germs, have beaten them, and be able to recognize most of them if they come around again. But a newborn's immune system just doesn't know very many germs yet. So almost every germ that comes along for the first time is allowed in. That's why kids always seem to be sick.

And another thing: if the membranes in my old schnozola swell one millimetre, it really doesn't matter because the thing is so big. (It's something I should visit one of my colleagues about one day.) In a tiny child's nose, however, one millimetre all around practically blocks the whole thing. Therefore, any mucus that's made in the nose only has one exit – out the front. Charming, isn't it?

Kids just don't come with adult nasal equipment. Their sinuses aren't formed until their skulls are large enough to accommodate them; thus children develop sinuses at different times in their lives. If they don't have the sinus problems that you and I have, this is merely because of their physical size.

Young children are tiny creatures and all of their airways are tiny – not just their noses but their tracheae and their bronchial trees as well. This gives rise to a whole bunch of problems such as croup (once again, the result of swelling membranes in small passageways) that keep parents awake at night. But as the children grow, the various air passageways become larger and swelling makes less of a difference. You hear about children "growing out of it." Well, they really do.

One of the conditions of having kids is that you're going to have them with stuffy noses a fair portion of the time, especially when they go to day care or start school. Those first years of group exposure are dynamite! You can't stop them from catching a runny nose. In fact they *need* to catch it – they're going to have to develop a sophisticated immune system sooner or later.

Once your child is all snuffed up, there are several things you can do. But perhaps I should first mention what you shouldn't do: rely on adult decongestants. They can send some little kids haywire. Instead of the sleepy child you expected, you might find yourself with one who's "hyper." You're better off with long-lasting paediatric nose drops, decongestants designed specifically for kids. Ask your pharmacist to help you choose the right one.

Another way to ease your child's discomfort is to make sure her bedroom is quite humid. A humidifier or a vaporizer left on overnight in the bedroom will help a lot. Moisture taken in from the air is good for a stuffy nose. But don't jump to the conclusion that moisture taken internally will be just as good. What your child drinks will be reflected in her urinary output, not her nasal output.

Remember, a runny nose alone isn't usually a serious symptom of disease. It's just a symptom of being a kid.

CAN A COLD BECOME PNEUMONIA?

C atching a cold is bad enough, but going bobsledding when you've got a cold? Well, honey, you're *bound* to get pneumonia. At least that's what your mother will say. She might add, "Serve you right, too."

Mom may be wrong, but she's got some good reasons for thinking that way. Sometimes, for an unlucky few, the symptoms of pneumonia start off resembling the symptoms of a cold. But most of the time, a cold is just a cold and will never grow up to be a more serious disease.

Pneumonia is an inflammation of the lung. A cold is an inflammation of the nasal airway. Pneumonia comes from a list of causes as long as your arm, but far and away the most common are infective viruses and bacteria. The virus that gives you a cold *can* give you pneumonia, but it usually doesn't.

The best way to catch pneumonia, should you for some unimaginable reason wish to do so, is to wait for the bug to catch you. Following a cold, when you have excess mucus in your nasal passages and lungs, you can breed pneumonia germs. This is known as a secondary infection. But you can't catch pneumonia by going out with a cold, with wet hair or without your jacket buttoned up. When Mom told you these "facts," she was saying what she believed, but Mom was misinformed.

Don't get me wrong: pneumonia can be a very serious disease. It can kill you. In the "good old days," one of the symptoms associated with it was delirium. When your temperature went high enough and you were sick enough, the functioning of your brain was affected.

Yet we don't hear as much about pneumonia these days. It is not the spectre of death that it was thirty or forty years ago, especially for children. Today, pneumonia is usually treated in the doctor's office – something that even physicians couldn't have imagined decades ago. Now it seems so simple: the patient comes in and the doctor prescribes the appropriate antibiotics.

Antibiotics have revolutionized the treatment of pneumonia. Not only is the patient not hospitalized, but he or she may not miss much more than a few days of school or work. The treatment is good; as a result far fewer people die from the disease.

You might still be afraid of something called "double pneumonia." My father got double pneumonia and almost died. My wife's grandfather got double pneumonia as a young man and did die. Double pneumonia was a devastating illness. It still can be if left untreated.

Double pneumonia is caused by pneumococcus, a particular kind of bacteria. Pneumococcus can ravage your lungs in twenty-four hours. This pneumonia is called "double" because it often hits both lungs at the same time. By the time it is diagnosed, it is tearing right through both lungs, filling them with fluid and mucus. In the "good old days" a person could die within forty-eight hours. Nowadays, if someone gets double pneumonia, penicillin or another broad-spectrum antibiotic will ensure he will be on the road to recovery within forty-eight hours. Most of the time no hospital admission is required. The difference antibiotics have made is dramatic: a very serious illness has become almost trivial.

So if you catch a cold, treat it as a cold and don't worry about it becoming an entirely different disease. There is, after all, a cure for pneumonia. But there still isn't a cure for a cold.

VITAMIN C: THE MIRACLE CURE?

When you feel a cold coming on, do you pop a hefty dose of Vitamin C? Most people think it helps. Are they deluding themselves?

Yes, but not very seriously. I'm uncomfortable rejecting Vitamin C therapy: it's an entirely harmless pastime and if it brings people comfort, I'm in favour of it. But if you want to know whether I think it's really effective, I'm afraid I have to say no.

Vitamin C enjoys widespread popularity. "I took it," people say, "and I got better. Ergo: it must have brought about the improvement." But that's not scientific proof. The few scientific studies carried out on the subject point the other way entirely. One of the best was done in Toronto by Dr. Terence Anderson, a professor of preventive medicine and public health. He concluded that Vitamin C did not reduce the incidence or length of colds.

Most people take Vitamin C on the well-why-not? principle. They may have the impression that they've shortened the number of days they're ill but, of course, there is no "control" – there's nobody else having the exact same cold and not taking Vitamin C.

The problem is the natural variability in the course of a cold. It depends mostly upon our previous immune experience. If we have met that class of virus before, we will have some immunity. So we might be sick for only twenty-four hours. But if we're not immune at all, the cold might last two weeks. Our immunity to cold viruses is not permanent as it is for smallpox or chicken-pox or many other illnesses.

If you get a short cold and happen to take some Vitamin C when you feel it coming on, then if you're feeling better in a day or two, you'll credit the Vitamin C.

Vitamin C is an extremely beneficial vitamin, there's no question about that. It saves lives and cures disease. But somehow, certain people have decided it's a cure for everything – including the common cold. They tend to take the conclusions of experimental studies and use them as a springboard for their own theories.

Maybe because there is no cure for the common cold, Vitamin C has been embraced as the next best thing. One of the hardest things for people to say is, "I've got a cold and I'm stuck with it for the duration." We all like to feel in charge of our lives. Taking a dose of Vitamin C makes us feel we're doing *something* about the situation.

At least you can't do yourself any harm. Because Vitamin C is water-soluble, you don't store it up uselessly as you can with fat-soluble vitamins. If you take a large dose of Vitamin C, you'll pee most of it out within four to six hours.

I can't offer any other nostrums for a cold. The only way to get through it is to take care of yourself. That includes, first and foremost, keeping your respiratory membranes moist, which means sticking close by a humidifier or vaporizer. That might be the best reason to stay home from the office, especially if the air is dry where you work. In addition you can use a decongestant to make yourself more comfortable, preferably one that doesn't make you dozy. Nose drops also give good relief.

So snuggle up with a good book for as long as it takes. This, too, shall pass.

BUT THERE'S ALWAYS CHICKEN SOUP

Everyone knows there *is* in fact a cure for the common cold. It's chicken soup!

I'm not willing to admit that good, old-fashioned chicken soup has all the healing properties of penicillin, but I will admit it definitely is good for you when you have a cold. No, it doesn't make the cold go away, but it will make you feel better. Not because it's chicken soup, but because it's nourishment.

When you have a cold or the flu, your whole body hurts. Your muscles, your bones, everything is really sick. It affects every cell in your body, including your gut – and that makes you temporarily anorexic.

You simply have no appetite. During the first day or two of an illness, some people don't eat anything. So besides feeling crummy from the illness, they feel even crummier because they need food and don't know it. If I can entice them to eat anything (and Mom's chicken soup sounds good to me), it will make them feel a whole lot better.

When you're sick, if you eat too much, you'll only upset your stomach. The trick is to eat small amounts frequently. Forget the three square meals. Sips of delicious broth go down very nicely, thank you.

The other benefit of chicken soup is that it is a liquid. If you're not drinking or eating enough because you've lost your appetite, you can experience fluid deprivation. Fluids are especially important with a cold because you need to keep your various juices flowing, especially those in the mucous membrane.

The mucous membrane moving in your lungs cleans things out. Without that flushing action, you're more prone to secondary infections. Keeping it working requires lots of fluids.

So go on – have a bowl of chicken soup. Add some rice, or noodles, or matzoh balls. Eat. Enjoy. It's good for you.

CHAPTER FOUR

YOU ARE
what You Eat

WHAT'S AT STEAK ON YOUR CHILD'S PLATE?

What do you do when the kid won't eat his peas or his Brussels sprouts or even (God forbid) the fettucine Alfredo? Well, you take heart – as long as he eats the meat, you're okay. At least, that's what a lot of parents think. But is it really true?

Let's separate the meat (ahem) from the chaff. I think meat is one of our least important foods. Nutritionally, we can do without meat more easily than we can do without lots of other parts of our diet.

Meat is basically a source of protein and fat which can quite quickly be converted into calories in our body through our metabolic machinery. But, quite frankly, we don't really need all the protein and fat we get in a North American diet. Less than thirty per cent of our dietary intake should be from animal sources.

There's quite a bit of truth in the idea that we are what we eat. Many things that happen to us in life have nothing to do with what we eat, of course, but some do. Hardening of the arteries and certain bowel diseases such as diverticulosis are partly a result of our diets. We can try to avoid these illnesses in a variety of ways, but until we really learn to manage what we eat, we'll never really get to the bottom of them.

Meat is neither essential to the human diet nor, in large quantities, is it good. So why does the human animal crave meat? Why weren't we satisfied with the vegetables that had adequately sustained us early on in our evolution?

The fact is, we evolved into omnivores – we eat a wide spectrum of foods. There are a couple of reasons why we like meat. Until fairly recently, meat was very expensive, in short supply, and difficult to come by. It was considered the food of the wealthy. So, as our living standards rose, everyone wanted to eat like kings – if it was expensive, it had to be good.

Meat is also a very satisfying source of calories. It sticks to your ribs, so to speak. When you've had a nice, fatty piece of meat, you feel really full and satisfied. And you get more calories in fewer grams of food because it's more concentrated. Fats have about thirty per cent more calories per weight than any other form of intake. Man the gatherer may have become man the hunter because meat was a more efficient meal.

There's no doubt we need protein, but we don't need much fat. There are endless sources of protein that are an alternative to red meat. Fish and fowl are both less fatty. Chicken still has a bit of fat to it, but a lot less than a T-bone. And fish is as streamlined as you can get.

Protein can be found in all sorts of seeds and grains. Bread and pasta are made with grains that contain five to eight percent protein, but they are lacking in certain vital amino acids. Legumes are also deficient in some amino acids but different ones, so a combination of grain and legume dishes will provide a full complement. Peas and beans are the most common legumes and up to thirty per cent of their total mass is protein. Even the humble potato has a two to three per cent protein content.

When your child eats meat and nothing else, you're teaching him bad dietary habits. It's a bad bargain to make in the power struggle every parent encounters with a child over food. You're teaching him meat is the most important part of the meal.

There are two ways to teach a child good eating habits. The first is by example. If you tell him to eat his spinach as you tuck into a one-inch thick steak that extends across your plate, obviously your actions will speak louder than your words.

The other way is to pay some attention to the way you present foods. People spend a lot of time thinking of new and interesting ways to dress up a meat dish, and then just plunk the peas or corn on the plate beside the "main" attraction. So try to think up attractive ways to sell the greens as well as the meat. You might also try serving your family an occasional meatless meal – a vegetable casserole or a pasta dish with a zesty tomato sauce. This will reinforce the idea that meat doesn't have to be the be-all and end-all of a dinner.

I can't guarantee that this approach might not run aground on the hard rocks of parenthood. Sometimes a kid just won't eat his vegetables.

Power struggles seem to be a natural part of having children. And one thing every parent can count on in a showdown over food: the child always wins. Try to lose as gracefully as possible.

One solution is to give the kid little choice on his plate and wait until he's really hungry. Starve 'em into submission! If he's been out in the playground all afternoon and he's ravenous, all of a sudden the vegetable he hated yesterday goes down lickety-split.

Unless, of course, it's asparagus. Every kid knows that asparagus tastes like rhinoceros toes.

WEIGHT WATCHERS' WOES

There are so many myths about dieting I don't know where to begin. It's like shooting ducks in a gallery. So let's aim at three in particular.

The first is the myth of the single item diet: that if you eat only one food, be it grapefruit or bananas, liquid protein or red meat, the pounds will miraculously melt away. The single item diets *are* valuable because only one thing over a period of time becomes intolerable. After a while you just can't stand that one food any more, so you will lose some weight simply because you eat less. I love grapefruit, but I couldn't take twenty-five a day.

Okay, let's say it does work and you lose a few pounds. Then what happens? You go back to eating a variety of foods and everything tastes so wonderful by comparison that you gorge and gain back every last ounce.

On this type of diet, along with eating the One Magic Food, you also drink a great deal of water because, invariably, the instructions for the diet say, "Eat only guacamole with ten glasses of water a day." There is some merit in that. But it has nothing to do with "flushing things out." Water simply keeps your stomach distended making you feel full and lowering your hankering for more food to put in it. So it does have some effect, but certainly not the commonly held belief that it washes calories away.

Patients trying to lose weight often ask their doctor for diuretics, or water pills. Water pills, whether you're trying to lose weight or not, are good for a couple of pounds or one kilogram. They do work up to a certain point; you can wring water out of anybody. But your problem probably isn't one kilogram; your problem most likely is more like fifteen kilograms. And as soon as you stop taking the water pills, you'll gain that kilo right back.

You certainly don't want to take diuretics for the rest of your life. They can be dangerous. They can deplete the potassium in your body. They also have side-effects such as loss of libido and impotence in some people. They can cause food sensitivity and skin rashes. Not a pretty picture. Why put up with all this if you don't have to? Are two pounds really that important?

This brings up myth number two: that it's possible to diet painlessly and without ever feeling hungry. There are a few lucky souls for whom this is true, and more power to them, but the rest of us must suffer for beauty.

Weight loss is like a bank account in reverse. In a bank account, it's hard to build up a surplus. With weight, it's hard to spend the surplus. One pound of human fat is worth 3500 calories. To lose one pound, then, you have to have a net deficit of 3500 calories. That means, if you take in 4000 calories in one day, by the end of the day you will have had to burn off 7500 to not add a pound and to lose one more. If you're going to do that, you have to restrict your intake dramatically, especially if you have a sedentary lifestyle. You can burn it off through exercise – but either way, you're going to feel hungry.

It is possible to lose weight without exercise. Your caloric needs will vary, depending on your sex, size, and occupation. A husky ditchdigger may need 3000 calories a day; a small-boned secretary may require only 1500. So if she limits her intake to 1000 calories, she's going to lose weight. Mind you, it will take at least a week to build up a net deficit of 3500 calories, and lose one pound of fat.

You'd think that, if your body really needs only 1500 calories a day, you wouldn't crave any more than that and wouldn't build up the surplus to begin with. But eating is habitual. I feel hungry first thing in the morning, at noon and at suppertime. I never eat between meals. And between six o'clock at night and seven the following morning, I will not eat anything and I will not feel hungry for the entire period of thirteen hours. But between eight a.m. and noon, a period of only four hours, I may feel hungry. In some cultures, people eat only two meals a day and don't feel hungry in between.

Some people say that's bad. They say eating large amounts in one sitting is what causes our weight problems. They recommend eating small amounts frequently. This recent fad, known as "grazing," is certainly very appealing. It seems to make sense to survive on little nibbles as the fancy strikes you. It is also an ideal way to lose track of your caloric intake. Some obese people can "graze" up to 6000 calories in one day and say, "But doctor, I never have a real meal. So how can I be fat?" The equation is simple: calories in must equal calories out.

The last duck in this gallery of diet myths is sugar substitutes. Every ten years or so, someone markets a wonderful new substance that will solve all our problems. In 1953, it was cyclamates. In 1963, it was saccharin. In 1974, it was aspartame.

Sugar substitutes can be helpful in a diet. They can provide oral gratification without adding calories. It's good to sip on a diet soda rather than swallow a candy. But they are not a total solution. One bite of a potato can undo an entire can of diet soda.

Cyclamates were banned in 1969 because they were linked to bladder tumours in rats. In 1977, there was a similar scare about saccharin. The final verdict isn't in on aspartame. I'm a bit wary of sugar substitutes – not as wary as I am of a lot of other drugs we use that we know are a clear and present danger. But generally speaking, sugar substitutes have not been tested for the effects in humans of large doses over long periods. They are being tested right now, in the marketplace. And that's the wrong place to test them.

I'm not a fan of sugar, but people make the mistake of thinking they can lose weight simply by removing all sugar from their diet. Your body is a huge sugar factory. It turns fats, protein, and carbohydrates into sugar. There's just no getting away from it.

WANTIN' WONTON

Imagine sitting in a Chinese restaurant at the end of a satisfying meal. You open up your fortune cookie and read: "In one hour, you will be hungry again." It sounds like another silly myth. But the fortune cookie is right.

Chinese food is different from the food Westerners usually eat. Our food is quite heavy in fats and proteins. But look at the next plate of Chinese food you get: there's just a bit of meat, and most of it in slivers, not big slabs. Also there's very little fat or oil. It's the fats and the protein that give you a heavy, full feeling. They take longer to process. You actually empty your stomach into the small bowel much more slowly. So the feedback from your stomach that it is full actually does last longer. With Chinese food, your stomach doesn't stay stretched out as long because the chopped-up vegetables and little bits of meat do work their way into the small bowel more quickly.

I also have a theory about the way Chinese food is served. I'm not sure it's even a little bit scientific, but I'll trot it out anyway.

The North American way of eating is to work through one or two courses and then stop for a breath. We receive signals from our insides saying, "That's enough, thank you," and we know we don't need any more meat and potatoes. So we slip into a nice 700-calorie dessert for a change of pace. We say we're "packing in around the corners." In fact, I hate to tell you, it's being packed in straight up front and centre.

When the Chinese sit down to eat, they go through a multi-course meal. But it's all spread out at once on the table, country-style. When you go to a Chinese restaurant, you don't usually have one dish, you have several. You think you've finished your "main course," but the waiter will gladly tell you you've just been through seven courses. You know by then you're full. And you've had enough variety that you don't feel a need for dessert.

Chinese food is a very well-balanced diet. It's probably a better-balanced diet than ours. We would do well to eat fewer fats and proteins by eating Chinese-style more often. A billion Chinese can't all be wrong.

CHILLING THE CHILI

The wonderful thing about living in a big city is the choice of food available. Anyone with taste and discernment can occasionally tuck into a taco or curry favour at the local Indian restaurant. But can everyone's stomach take it? Many claim the chilis start a fire in their insides.

The heartburn is due partly to the spices – and partly to your past experience with hot food. When I was doctoring in Nigeria, I ate some of the hottest food I have ever had in my life. In the remote area where I was practising, the people garnished their food with little peppers they gathered from the bush. And they were *hot*. I used to call them dehydrated fire – if you add water, they burst into flame. So drinking after you bit into one of these babies didn't help. It actually made it worse.

I was very flattered when, shortly after my wife and I arrived in town, I received my first invitation to dine at the home of one of the locals. I was very interested in finding out what and how the Nigerians ate.

Our hosts presented me with a tiny fish, about two fingers long. It just lay in the dish and certainly did not look very appetizing to my Western eyes. I bit into it and discovered ... dehydrated fire! Eating it was almost impossible; but I ate it, I suffered, I smiled. I tried to behave like a good guest. I tried to share it with others, but no one else would have any.

By the time I got home, I was in such pain that my ears ached. And my stomach hurt. The next morning, I hurt farther on down because it had explosive effects as it exited. But even more shocking was that, when I looked in the mirror, I saw that my mouth had been burned. It was blistered, and the skin was literally beginning to hang in shreds. I thought perhaps dinner the night before was really some sort of wild initiation stunt for the new doctor. But I learned soon enough that that's the way the Nigerians really do eat their food.

By the time I left Nigeria several months later, I could eat all the local dishes with no problems. They caused me no indigestion, caused me no pain. I rather liked them. In fact, when I got home I realized that some of the things we consider hot here aren't all that hot by comparison. "Hot" depends a lot on what you're accustomed to.

What people who are raised on spicy foods get accustomed to are the chemicals in the spices that are capable of irritating our skin tissue as well as causing acid secretion in the stomach. If you want to eat spicy foods without spending years acclimatizing your body to these chemicals, you can use antacids to coat your stomach before you bite into the chilis. And, if your stomach still feels rough the morning after, pop some more to calm it down. Antacids will help but they definitely won't solve the whole problem: your mouth will still be just as scorched!

Most of the commercial antacids on the shelf at your local drugstore are up to the job. The one exception is any antacid which contains calcium carbonate. By law, the ingredients in any remedy must be listed on the label. So read before you buy. Stay away from the calcium carbonate because it can cause a rebound hyperacidity about an hour to an hour-and-a-half after you take it. You are then caught in a vicious cycle: taking medicine to relieve what you previously took it for. Tablet-form antacids are usually the ones to be wary of. Most of the liquid preparations do not contain calcium carbonate because it's not very soluble.

Some people recommend milk or cream, which, traditionally, has been used as a buffer. This works fairly well, but not for everyone. Milk and cream also contain a fair bit of calcium, and it's the calcium that can cause the rebound hyperacidity.

One mistake people make when they want to douse the fire within is to avoid drinking fruit juice. They believe that fruit juice contains citric acid which will only aggravate the problem. Acid is acid, right? Wrong. Citric acid is a very weak acid compared to the hydrochloric acid in your stomach. Fruit juice contains fruit salts, which are excellent buffering agents, capable of absorbing a lot of strong acids.

So a glass of refreshing grapefruit or orange juice can indeed put out the flames.

The debate about the right drink to accompany the hot stuff burns on. Some fire-eaters swear by tea, others by beer or dry cider. It doesn't make any difference what you drink – the relief is only temporary.

You don't feel the heat when you first bite into something hot. You might have even swallowed it and be on your second mouthful before it hits. The reason is quite simple: the chemicals released from the chili or spices take a while to seep through the layers of tissue in your mouth. It's not until they have literally soaked in and stimulated the nerve endings that you feel that burning sensation. We talk about something tasting hot, but it's not really the sense of taste that's at work here. Your sense of taste works immediately; the sensation of burning builds up slowly. There may actually be a lag time of half a minute or a minute between your first bite and the afterburner feeling which continues to build.

Once the heat is in your mouth, how do you get it out? Not easily. A sip of tea or beer or cider will wash away only what's on the surface of the inside of your mouth, but it's not what's on the surface that's causing you grief. It's what's already seeped into the flesh. It will wear off with time, but chances are you will have taken another bite before then. Rinsing it away between bites is a good idea, but not The Solution.

A couple of things can ease the pain, at least in your mouth. Yoghurt can feel smooth and cool on the rough edges forming and, because it's solid, it stays in your mouth longer than milk. Bread can soak up the hot oils the peppers give off as you chew. But once the hot stuff gets down to your stomach, the bread and yoghurt can't help you there. It's time to call the fire department.

MY HICCUP RUNNETH OVER

Suppose you've got the hiccups. Here's what you do: you take a glass of water, put your lip on the rim farthest away from you, and then you bend over and drink. Now you're probably all wet, but at least you're rid of those troublesome hiccups.

There are as many folk cures for hiccups as there are folks. Everybody's got a favourite way of getting rid of them. And some methods do work.

Why people get the hiccups is not perfectly understood. But I can describe how it happens. We all have a diaphragm, a big sheet of strong muscle that separates the contents of our chest from the contents of our abdomen. The diaphragm is controlled by the phrenic nerve. Our innards, the abdominal contents, have another nerve called the vegas nerve. These two nerves connect to a common area in the brain. They might get their signals crossed and set up a cycle between them which results in a purposeless contraction of the diaphragm. Once it starts, it continues rhythmically and we're off – hic, pause, hic, pause, hic, pause .... It's a little joke between your abdomen and your diaphragm.

It's usually funny unless you get a really bad case; then it's somewhat less humorous. Once in a while people get pernicious hiccups which most frequently occur with cancer patients. For them, this is actually a medical disaster. Hiccups are tolerable for a half day or so, but if they last longer than that they become an exhausting, draining process that interrupts sleep, makes eating difficult, makes all of life difficult and becomes an acute form of torture. Fortunately, pernicious hiccups are rare, and ordinary hiccups in an otherwise healthy person don't amount to much more than a social discomfort.

One of the things that stimulates the vegas nerve is distension, or swelling, in the abdominal contents. If you've got a big bubble of gas in your stomach or in one loop of your bowel, it might send up signals of irritation that come bouncing back down the phrenic nerve and away (hic) you (hic) go!

When you take a glass of water and drink it upside-down, you might dislodge that bubble of gas, move it farther down the bowel, say, and relieve the tension. If it works for you, you'll swear that's the answer. Or you can try to get the bubble out the front end, so to speak, by belching. A good way to provoke a belch is to sit down and lean forward with your right elbow on your left knee. This position puts your body at a forty-five degree angle, which lines up your stomach with the esophagus and lets the bubble escape.

But let's say you just ate too much, and it's not a bubble of gas that's causing the hiccups. There's simply too much fuel and food in your belly. All the tricks won't do any good.

For severe hiccups, you can feed a catheter through your nose to the back of the throat and literally tickle the back of the throat. This will get your gag reflex going (not pleasant), and will interrupt the hiccups. It's a diversionary tactic.

A simpler thing to do, based on the same idea, is to swallow a bit of dry, white sugar. It's like swallowing a handful of sand, but it works because it abrades the back of your throat and sends up a counter-irritation.

A paper bag over your head? Sure, why not? Scaring the hiccups away with a loud noise? Okay, as long as the neighbours don't call the police. The reason so many folk remedies do get rid of hiccups is that they break the feedback cycle, the short-circuit between the phrenic and vegas nerves. No one's found one single foolproof method, but some of these antics can at least be amusing – as amusing as hiccups are to anyone who hasn't got them.

BEAUTY
is only Skin Deep

ITCHING FOR THE TRUTH

Is poison ivy contagious? This is frequently asked by parents of kids who've come home from the woods covered in itchy rashes. This is a trick question. When we think of contagion, we usually think of disease transmitted by germs. So poison ivy isn't contagious in the true sense of the word. But the bad news is: it *can* spread.

The poison ivy rash is the result of an allergic reaction to an oil on the surface of the leaves of the poison ivy plant. This oil, needless to say, is transmittable, as any oily substance is, from one surface to another. If you have the oil on your skin and touch someone else, or if you touch the arm of a chair, for example, and leave enough there for it to rub off on someone else, you could "spread" poison ivy.

The problem is that the reaction most people get to poison ivy takes time to show up. The oil has to seep into your flesh just below the level of the skin before your antibodies charge up to defend your system. It is an unfortunate combination of your own antibodies with this foreign invader that ultimately results in inflammation and weeping blisters. The process could take days to develop. The rash itself is certainly not contagious, and by the time it shows up, you don't have any of the plant's oils on the exterior of your skin to pass on in a handshake or a hug.

There are a lucky few who don't have an immune reaction to the oils in the plant. To them, poison ivy is just another leaf. But if you know you are sensitive and you come into contact with poison ivy, you should head immediately for the nearest bar – of soap.

Just as after working on your car, you need lots of soap to get rid of the oil on your hands, you need several good lathers to make sure you get the poison ivy oil off your skin. If you wash thoroughly enough, there's a good chance you'll get rid of it all and avoid the allergic reaction.

People who have never experienced a poison ivy reaction tend to be unsympathetic to a sufferer simply because they don't realize how bad it can be. We've all had an itch. We've all had a mosquito bite or a mild rash, and we know that an itch can be an annoyance. But until you've had poison ivy, you don't know what an itch is. The itch of poison ivy can be so bad you can't think of anything else. You can't sleep properly; you don't eat well; you don't work well – your whole life is consumed by the itch. It can just about drive you crazy. You have got to do something about it.

For a fairly mild case, cortisone creams do provide some relief. So do cold packs, but they are temporary. For a bad case, oral cortisone may be necessary. Cortisone is a very powerful drug fraught with the possibility of side-effects, but it is relatively safe used for the short-term in high doses that taper off rapidly. On balance, it is the best thing to deliver people from the terrible misery poison ivy can create.

By now you've probably realized I have a personal interest in the subject. Once you've had poison ivy, you develop a certain passion about it. Every time you go to a forest, you look for that three-leaved plant. The forest is full of similar-looking plants, but once you've been bitten, so to speak, you can pick it out on the forest floor as if it were lit in neon. I have had poison ivy. I have had it so severely that it made my life impossible. I am a conservationist when it comes to plants and animals. But when it comes to poison ivy, uprooting every last plant would be too kind an end.

THE BURNING QUESTION

Everyone's medicine chest probably contains an ointment that claims to be designed for minor burns. Folk wisdom tells us that when we burn ourselves, some sort of oily substance, be it good old-fashioned butter or an unpronounceable brand of cream in a tube should cover the burn to keep it from being exposed to air.

It's part of human nature to believe that we can do something better than Mother Nature can. But in this case, Mother Nature's way really is the best. Don't put anything on the burn. Leave it alone and it will do just fine, thank you.

There are two things that can happen when you burn yourself. One is that the layers of your skin will separate, the top layer will bubble up, and a fluid will leak out between the layers. This is a blister – something we've all experienced. It is sterile. The top is intact, impervious to bacterial penetration, and the liquid forms a good protective cushion. It's perfect! You couldn't design a better dressing for the wound.

Now, if the blister breaks, the skin underneath will ooze natural body fluids which, in a little while, will form a sterile crust. Once again, you can't do better. So leave the burn alone and let Mother Nature do her thing. When she's through, you might want to protect the burn from friction, from bumping into things and so forth, so you can add a dry dressing to top off her work. But for the first hour or two after you have been burned, don't interfere in the natural healing process.

We think ointments are a good idea because they provide temporary relief by excluding air from the wound. But when the effect of the ointment wears off, the pain will be just as great as it was before. And the big problem with ointments is that they soften the top of a blister and make it fragile enough to break from the least touch. To protect the wound, the blister needs to be dry on the outer surface. If you apply ointment after a blister has broken, it will prevent your own juices from forming a crust.

The other problem with an ointment, especially if it has been lying around the medicine chest for some time after being opened, is that you have no way of knowing if it is sterile. It probably isn't. Butter certainly isn't. And infection is the worst thing that can happen to a burn. A minor burn can become serious through infection.

One folk remedy that does have something to recommend it is putting the burn under cold water immediately. I can't guarantee the quality of water from the nearest pond, but tap water is sterile. It has several beneficial effects. First, it cools whatever is on the skin that is causing the burning sensation. If you can apply it within the first few seconds, it is extremely helpful and prevents the heat from spreading. Second, it numbs the skin so that you are less uncomfortable. And third, it causes your blood vessels to shrink and tighten up, reversing their natural tendency in a situation like this to dilate, open up, and start to leak fluids which cause swelling. Cold compresses applied for thirty minutes are ideal.

I know from personal experience that this works. I was on vacation with my family, all of us in the hotel coffee shop for breakfast, when a waitress spilled a pot of coffee down my six-year-old's back. There aren't supposed to be any surprises at a Holiday Inn, but all the patrons of the coffee shop certainly got one when my son let out a blood-curdling scream.

I knew we were in trouble. I reached behind me where I had noticed the ice water jugs were stored and I quickly up-ended one down the poor kid's back. His second scream was just as blood-curdling as his first.

I had realized that it was necessary to neutralize the hot with some cold right away. He was wearing a T-shirt and a sweater, and the fabrics, soaked in the hot liquid, were continuing to cook his flesh. It was important to cool off the clothes and get them off him right away.

Despite my best efforts, my son did wind up with a large superficial burn on his back and lost a huge slab of skin. It really put a stopper on our holiday. But cooling the area right away prevented the injury from becoming a deeper, third-degree burn that would have required skin grafts.

When I see patients who have been burned, it is the rare one who comes in *not* lathered with ointment. Everything you can imagine is put on burns, and the doctor's first job is to get that stuff off. If it is a water-based product, it simply soaks off with some saline solution. But if it's oil-based, it's a real problem because you don't want to use detergents and soaps on a fresh wound. Sometimes you try to scrape it off gently, or just put up with it, hoping it won't prevent the formation of a crust underneath. From a doctor's perspective, ointment is a real nuisance.

How did this notion of putting ointments on burns get started? Well, people know if you put water on a burn it does provide temporary relief. So they extend the idea: if something as simple as water helps, then something more complex must be even better. And, of course, advertising perpetuates this idea.

But I also think the notion comes from the fact that it's difficult for people to do *nothing* when they are hurt. If a doctor says, "Leave it alone," this sounds crazy. It hurts, and there must be something to relieve the pain. Waiting around for a blister or a crust to form and then merely putting a dry dressing on top takes discipline. When your kids come up to you with a burn and say, "Fix it," try advising restraint. Leave it alone you must.

If you need to do *something* while waiting around for the burn to heal, try screaming. Make those around you suffer with you. And if you want to put your mouth to good use, take an effective oral pain killer, but don't touch that burn.

CHOCOLATE LOVERS UNITE!

Is a Mars Bar called a Mars Bar because eating it makes your face look like the planet? I believed this way back when I was a zitty teenager.

I had a bad case of acne, the kind that makes your face look like an exploded bombshell. It was extremely depressing for my fragile ego in those early years. I was told that if I cut out chocolate and Coke and other wicked things, the problem would go away. So I did. I was highly motivated. I was determined to look like a real person, not an unpaved road.

After six months of deprivation, things weren't any better. So I decided the whole idea was crazy. I have remained convinced this myth is a pock-faced lie ever since. No one should take it seriously. The whole time I was in medical school, the subject never came up once.

On the surface, the idea that chocolate gives you pimples *seems* to make sense. I had been told (before I knew to argue about it) that chocolate and nuts and other goodies of that ilk are bad for the complexion because they are very oily. There certainly is oil in the cocoa bean and in a hazel nut and on potato chips. So it would make sense that these oils added to the oil already on your skin will make pimples spring up like dandelions on a lawn.

But stop and think: is there any more oil in a chocolate bar than in milk, eggs, cheese, or butter? When was the last time you heard a parent say, "Don't drink that milk! It will give you zits!"?

I think this myth grew out of a puritan mentality that says if there's something wrong with us, we must be doing something to deserve it. And if we deny ourselves sinful pleasures, we will improve. It's hard for a parent to look at a spotty-faced kid and say, "That's just the way it is, folks." And knowing how repulsive teenage eating habits can be, we make junk food a convenient scapegoat.

So where do pimples come from? Obviously, from under your skin. Your hair grows out of follicles, and each follicle is connected by a long duct to an oil gland. The oil gland does not empty directly onto the surface of the skin. The oil passes through the duct alongside the hair follicle and spreads from there. But sometimes the oil dries up at the opening to the follicle and forms a little plug. You don't really see it at first because it's colourless. Often it will get squeezed out naturally. But if it stays there, it oxidizes and turns into a blackhead.

Meanwhile, back at the oil factory the gland doesn't know the opening is blocked. It keeps producing oil. The oil keeps flowing into the duct and up to the follicle, which starts to swell.

Then the bacteria start to get into the act. They are capable of turning the normal oils on the skin into fatty acids. It's the fatty acids that are very irritating and cause the inflammation we call a pimple. The result is red-hot, big, vicious bumps that can sometimes become abscessed.

No one knows for sure why teenagers are so prone to this

phenomenon. We do know that it is related to hormone levels in the body, especially the male hormone. And, of course, teenage bodies experience huge surges in hormones.

Male and female bodies each have both male and female hormones. In the teenage years, the balance between the male and female hormones is often askew. It would be simple to speculate that a young woman with complexion problems may have an over-production of male hormones. But it doesn't seem to be the case. A woman who gets pregnant, for example, is definitely producing more female hormones than male, yet she might suddenly develop a case of acne. Or, if she's had pimples before, the pregnancy might clear up her complexion. Sometimes young women go on the Pill just to solve their skin problems. Some get better, others get worse.

The one characteristic pimple-sufferers all share is an oily skin. They will wash their faces completely free of oils at 8 a.m., and by 11 have skin that is positively slippery and shiny. They are hyper-secreters of oil.

The remedies for zits haven't changed much since the bad old days when I had them. People still rely on drying agents, soaps, and detergents that literally strip off the oil accumulated on the skin. There are also stronger drying agents that will peel off the dried or dead layers of skin. They do work. Some are available over-the-counter, but the more potent ones require a prescription.

Benzoil peroxide is one of these cleansing agents found in many over-the-counter products. Precipitated sulphur is another. They come in various strengths which should be marked on the label and work by lifting off the dead layers of skin so that they can't combine with the oil in the follicle to form plugs.

Antibiotics have been used for twenty years or more with considerably good results for some people. Tetracycline is the most common type. It seems to affect the actual production of oil in the skin as well as kill off the bacteria that turn the oil into fatty acids. But antibiotics are not the best long-term treatment. They do have side-effects. For example, tetracycline taken by pregnant women is known to affect tooth development in a fetus.

For very severe cases of acne, there are some promising new treatments. Acutane, a distant relative of Vitamin A, has been getting good reports. There is a high incidence of side-effects, and for pregnant women it has proven to be devastating. It is a medication that should never be passed on to help out a friend who has a few zits. But for a young man or woman whose life is being ruined by mounds of unattractive acne, this may literally be a face saver.

I can't guarantee that getting rid of the zits will swing your love life into high gear. But at least if you're sitting home mending a broken heart, you can dip into the chocolate box for consolation without worrying that you'll wind up showing your indulgence on your face.

BAKED, BROILED, FRIED AND GRILLED

The sun's out. It's time to do your George Hamilton imitation. If you think you can go out to bask armed simply with some baby oil or cocoa butter against a potential burn, you'd better whoa up there, Paleface.

Unfortunately, this myth is still believed by many people. Advertisements for these products never actually claim sunburn protection but they don't seem to mind implying it – with no scientific basis.

A sunburn (and a tan, for that matter) is caused by ultraviolet light from the sun. The more ultraviolet light that hits your skin the more you are going to burn. If you want to avoid burning, you have to block out the ultraviolet light. And the simple truth is that baby oil and cocoa butter don't block ultraviolet light. But if you're going to fry, I suppose you might as well fry in oil or butter.

Suntan *lotions*, on the other hand, can block out the harmful rays. Many of them are excellent products. I use them myself, but I would never buy one that didn't carry a number rating on it. These numbers tell you how much sunburning resistance the lotion contains. A two or a six or a fifteen on the label means there is enough sunburn protection in the product to allow you to remain in the sun two, six or fifteen times as long as you could without protection.

But be careful! You can still get scorched. The numbers are guidelines, not promises. If you apply a four the first day out in the sun, you might think you can stay out for an hour instead of fifteen minutes. But for pale skin, it's not enough protection. You really should start out with the highest number and work slowly towards a lower one. Even a fifteen is not a total block. But it will allow you to tan gradually, the proper way to get a tan.

If, in spite of these precautions, you still get a sunburn, there are ways to take care of it. But the old home remedy, vinegar, is not one I would recommend.

If your sunburn is peeling and cracked, vinegar, even diluted, can have a noxious effect. It is true that vinegar does have a cooling effect on burning skin, but unless you're planning to dive into a salad bowl, it's not the most appetizing treatment.

Oils and moisturizing lotions do have a soothing effect because they make your skin feel less tight. But they don't have any real effect on your body's own efforts to heal the burn. They can be a hazard if your burn has turned into blisters and any of them are weeping. Applying oils or lotions to skin in this condition could open the way for infection.

Applying a natural product, such as the liquid extracted from the aloe, does bring comfort, and it has one advantage: if you extract it yourself, chances are the liquid is fairly sterile because it comes from the pith of the plant, not the surface. A lot of people swear by it, and I'm not about to argue with them.

Technology, as usual, has an answer: a spray that claims to contain an anaesthetic. It will give you temporary relief but not because of the anaesthetic. It is the fact of spraying that cools you off – the spray is highly volatile and by evaporating quickly, creates a cooling sensation. The anaesthetic itself is probably psychotherapy: if you think it helps, it probably does. To be really effective, it would have to reach the nerve endings below the surface of your skin, which is a fairly impenetrable barrier; unless the skin is blistered and weeping, the anaesthetic won't get through to the nerve endings. And if your skin is blistered and weeping, applying a spray is just as dangerous as applying a lotion or oil.

To take care of a sunburn properly, first get out of the sun. Unfortunately, people think that as long as they cover the sunburned parts, they can continue to fry the rest of their body. This is not so.

You need time to heal. Cold compresses or a cool bath will help. A severe sunburn is a form of illness. You could feel feverish, nauseated, lethargic. It is not your imagination. You are ill. So you need rest and something such as Tylenol to bring down the fever just as you would with any other disease. I don't mean to sound alarmist, but people don't seem to realize how serious a sunburn can be. Some cases need to be hospitalized. Fortunately that's rare – but it does happen.

Sunburn also has some serious long-term effects which aren't properly understood. For example, the effects of ultraviolet radiation are cumulative over a lifetime. The sunburn you got at fifteen is added on to the one you had at twenty-five, and both will be added on to the one you get at fifty.

The more deeply ultraviolet rays penetrate into the skin, the more damage they do. Fair-haired and fair-skinned people are usually the most at risk. The more transparent the skin, the more ultraviolet light can get right through to the basal areas of the skin and into the subcutaneous tissue.

The effects don't take all that long to be seen. Fair-haired and fair-skinned people can look sun-damaged by the time they're in their twenties. Their skin is permanently reddened, flaky, and rough. Sometimes it looks as though they have little road maps across their faces from dilated vessels, perhaps across the upper cheek or across the nose. This is simply the cumulative affect of sun.

The next stage is pre-cancerous. Cancer of the skin is a very real problem. It takes a while to build up, but it's not unusual for sunworshippers in their fifties to walk into the doctor's office complaining of constant irritation on their faces.

Even if you avoid that drastic fate, staying out in the sun will still definitely harm your skin. It will age you prematurely, cause unnecessary wrinkles and weakening of the tissue. If you wind up with a face by Gucci, don't expect your doctor to be able to fix it. The damage is irreparable.

THE FOUNTAIN OF YOUTH

The ads look convincing. A lovely model (who is probably eighteen years old) smoothes the miraculous new anti-wrinkle emulsion around her eyes where crow's feet would be if she were thirty years older. A mere seventy-five or a hundred dollars will buy you a fingernail's worth of the magic cream. It contains the most amazing anti-ageing compound ever discovered: collagen.

Collagen has been around as long as people and animals have existed. We've known about its chemical structure for about a hundred years. More recently, we have learned that changes in collagen are part of the ageing process. And it's never long from the discovery that something is part of some unpleasant process to some charlatan figuring out a way to make a buck on it.

We have collagen throughout our bodies in two forms, organized and disorganized. Organized collagen is in long strands lined up together to form a ligament or a tendon, very useful in holding our bones and muscles together. Disorganized collagen is underneath the skin. It is the subcutaneous tissue, a dense web that weaves everything together. If you cut the skin open, you can't see any individual strands; it courses through everything in random directions.

When we age, collagen changes as do other fibres called elastin. Their structure is altered – the reason our skin sags. Some factors can accelerate the process, especially smoking and sun-damage. A "smoker's face," characterized by crow's feet and lines around the mouth, is the result of smoking's effect on collagen.

Collagen treatments take two forms: creams applied to the skin and injections. The creams contain animal collagen, usually taken from cows.

If you want to buy the best collagen going, skip the cosmetics counter and go down to a woodworking shop for some hide glue. It's the purest collagen going, and it's used by old-fashioned woodworkers on joints. It's cheap and good, although it does tend to get brown and brittle. But if you want to rub collagen on your face, at least you know you've got a pure product.

The tiny vials with pretty packaging cost seventy-five to a hundred dollars for the simple reason that manufacturers can convince you they are worth it. There is no regulatory body for cosmetics, as there is for drugs, to insist a product has to work before it can be marketed. As long as it has been proved that it's not dangerous, anyone can ask a king's ransom for a product and get it if the pitch is good enough. It's really quite harmless – except to your pocketbook.

Rubbing collagen on your face just doesn't work. Your skin is an organ of covering; it is not an organ of digestion. It doesn't break molecules up, neither does it absorb them. Your skin is designed to keep the outside out and the inside in. That's why God put it there – and He knew what He was doing. If you believe that skin can absorb protein, then you'll also believe that wrapping a New York sirloin around your biceps will result in bigger muscles.

Collagen injections, on the other hand, do help cosmetic defects. If you have a deep pit on your face, caused by scarring after an accident or disease, it can be filled out by the injection of collagen that is sterile and chemically altered so that your body won't reject it as a foreign substance.

It is very beneficial in cases of disfiguring skin aberrations. For example, my brother-in-law suffered from shingles on his face when he was young. He grew up looking like the Pillsbury Doughboy and, needless to say, didn't have a very good time of it. He has been helped a great deal by collagen injections. They are expensive, and the effect is not permanent. But if you think in terms of saving face once every two or three years, it's definitely worth it.

Of course collagen shots are also available to serve the cause of vanity. There's nothing wrong, if you can afford it, in getting a few wrinkles plumped up with collagen so they are less visible. The collagen won't make the wrinkles go away, but it will fill the area out giving an over-all effect of smoothness. But remember that, with any injection, there is always a possibility of infection. And in rare cases, if you're sensitive to the substance, you could experience redness and swelling.

The next time you walk past a cosmetic counter, turn your nose up at the "Fountain of Youth" in a jar. I would never recommend anyone buy collagen cream – unless I had stocks in the company.

CHAPTER SIX

Out on a
LIMB

YOU'RE PULLING MY LEG

Anybody who has ever lugged a heavy suitcase through an airport knows that one arm is definitely longer than the other. If it wasn't when you started out, it is by the time you reach your destination. However, the word is that no matter what you've lugged or have not lugged, one arm really is usually longer than the other. The same is true of legs.

Don't adjust your mirror. Here, for a change, is a myth that's true. We are not exactly symmetrical creatures. We are nearly so, but not exactly. And this is perfectly normal unless, of course, one set of knuckles drags on the ground and the other doesn't.

The usual difference between one leg and another is one to two centimetres, or half an inch to one inch. One arm can vary from the other by up to one centimetre or half an inch. No wonder dressmakers go nuts!

From time to time, patients will come to see the doctor on the recommendation of a tailor. They've just been measured for clothes and discovered a whole inch needed to be added onto one sleeve or onto one pant leg.

Unless there's a really extreme difference, a doctor can't confirm the tailor's suspicions by simply looking the patient over. He needs to take a really good look. The best way to look would be with x-rays. The doctor measures carefully between bony prominences – from the pelvis to the knee, from the knee to the ankle. Not only can the doctor run a tape measure or ruler along the photos more accurately, he can also see if there are any problems in the bones that account for the discrepancy. But not everyone should have x-rays, certainly not just to satisfy their tailor's curiosity.

The difference in the length of your legs (if there is one) is blamed for all sorts of complaints. The most common one is lower back pain. People ask me, "Do you think the reason I'm having my back problem, doctor, is because one leg is longer than the other?" That's what their friends have told them. And, of course, if you measure very carefully, it becomes a self-fulfilling prophecy. They do have a back problem and, by golly, one leg is a centimetre longer than the other. But medically speaking, it doesn't follow.

A variation of limbs within the normal range doesn't do a person any harm. It might even have some advantages. You might be able to turn better when you ski or walk steadily on unsteady surfaces – as long as you go in only one direction. Think of it: on board a listing ship you can get to the fore more easily. You might never be able to go aft unless the ship lists the other way. Come to think of it, uneven legs are simply a one-way ticket.

Legs can be a measure of many things. Certain forms of dwarfism are manifested in the limbs rather than in the body. A person might have a normal trunk length but be short because of abnormally undersized legs.

On the other hand, some people have abnormally long legs. They're considered lucky because somewhere along the way our culture has decided that long legs are beautiful. They're certainly prized by dancers and dress designers.

A normal, well-proportioned person measures up surprisingly neatly. The distance from the pubic bone to the heel usually is the same as the distance from the pubic bone to the top of the head. We think of our "middle" as being our waist, but, geographically speaking, it's really about hip level.

Yet you'd never get the impression that these proportions are normal by looking at ads in the newspapers, especially the ones of a pretty young woman in the fashion pages. Check it out – she has been posed in the picture for effect, not accuracy and her legs seem anatomically speaking, proportionately wrong. They're far too long for her body. Consequently, instead of being fifty/fifty, she's twenty-five/seventy-five below the "middle." She's the odd woman out, yet she makes "normal" people feel inadequate.

The next time you wish that your legs started at your belly button, remember what Abraham Lincoln said when someone once asked him, "How long should a man's legs be?" Honest Abe didn't say, as I would be tempted to, "What a bizarre question!" He actually answered with one of the most medically sound statements I've ever heard. He said, "Long enough to reach the ground."

SPRAIN, SPRAIN, GO AWAY

If you have the bad luck to sprain your ankle, console yourself with this thought: at least you didn't break the bone. A fracture is always worse than a sprain. Or so people say.

The truth depends on what sort of sprain and what sort of break you're talking about. I'd say that sometimes a break is definitely preferable to a sprain. Some breaks heal more easily with less long-term effect than some sprains. At the risk of sounding more like a lawyer than a doctor, I'll have to say that there's a wide spectrum of breaks and an equally wide spectrum of sprains, and that the advantages of one type of injury over another are entirely relative.

Technically speaking, a sprain is an injury to the soft tissues around the joint. Your joint is held together by a capsular structure that includes ligaments and various retention muscles. All of these can be stretched and torn. Your whole joint can be disrupted so that you put it right out – better known as a dislocation. A break, on the other hand, doesn't usually occur at a joint and usually involves only the shaft of a bone.

Very often you can figure out after a fall what sort of injury you have. A minor sprain will not put you too badly out of commission. You've slightly stretched a few ligaments, the area swells up a bit and may be somewhat painful. If you can't move and the pain is very great, it's not so easy to tell if it's a break or a serious sprain. You will need to have x-rays to determine which it is because the symptoms are almost identical.

Both a break and a serious sprain can be very disabling in the long term. Both require prolonged convalescence.

People think a broken bone is serious, but they are wrong to consider sprains trivial by comparison. They think a sprain is a little twist that's sore for a while and needs three days or a week to get back to normal. But in fact some sprains might require a convalescence of four to six months and painful physiotherapy. And that's without any bones broken at all!

People also assume that a fracture requires a cast and a sprain does not. Wrong again. Your friends can Magic Marker their hearts out on your cast if you have a serious sprain. In fact, if you have a broken bone, there's no guarantee you will get to wear your badge of honour. These days, some fractures mend without any cast at all.

The cast you get for a serious sprain will look the same as one for a broken bone, but it has a different function. For one thing, it will stay on for a much shorter time. For a bone to heal, it needs to be kept still long enough for it to grow back together. Once it does, it's as solid as before. It doesn't have to do much but bear weight.

A joint, however, has to move. So, after some weeks in a cast to maintain alignment, the ligaments and joint capsule are going to have to learn to function again. They will be expected to stretch, twist, and move in all directions as well as bear weight. As soon as the cast is off, you have to begin a long and painful re-education before the ligaments are healed. If you let them sit idle too long, you could face a permanent disability. Things may be "frozen" and never move again. The timing of cast removal is always a delicate balance between too short and too long.

That's one of the critical differences between a sprain and a fracture. The other is the possibility of recurrence. Usually, once a bone heals, it's a pretty solid union which takes a very serious disruption to undo. Unstable fractures are not very common. But it is very common to have a recurring injury after a sprain. If the ligament isn't healed for long enough, or if it's not exercised properly, it will be weak and have a limited range of motion.

I'm sure you've heard people say, "You know, since I sprained my ankle, I do it every six months." They're not kidding. And they're not just clumsy, either. Their weak ligaments make them unsteady enough on their feet that even a crack in the sidewalk will do the trick. That's why no one in the theatre ever says "Sprain a leg!"

ROAD MAPS TO THE KNEECAPS

Have a care – have a chair. Don't stay on your feet, poor dear, or you'll wind up with varicose veins." Does this sound familiar?

It sounds familiar, all right. But it's misinformed. You do not get varicose veins from standing up too much. But if you already have varicose veins, it is true that standing a lot can make them feel worse. It can make your legs uncomfortable. It can make your legs swell. It can give you grief. But it does not cause them.

Varicose veins come mostly to those who inherit them, whether they spend their lives standing up or sitting down. "My grandmother had them, my mother had them, and now I have them," confides a patient. "Can this be genetic, doctor?" Yes, it usually is. Not in every case, but a genetic predisposition is usually the villain.

You see, your veins don't have a heart to pump the blood through them as an artery does. Blood goes down the arteries pushed by the pumping of your heart. It then goes through the capillary bed and comes back up through the veins. When it is coming back up from your legs, it's an uphill battle. You have no ticker, you may have noticed, in your toes.

What the veins do have to help them is muscle. As the blood travels up your leg, each muscle contraction gives a leg up, so to speak, along the way. Your veins also have a series of valves in them that form a sort of ladder. As the blood is pushed up over a rung, it stays in the valve waiting for the next muscle squeeze. Gradually, it makes it all the way back to the heart.

Some people, unfortunately, are born with either too few valves or valves that don't work properly. When their blood is pushed up, their valves aren't on the job and it just sloshes back down when the pressure's off.

If the blood keeps flushing back down and hammering on the vein walls, sooner or later the veins will get weak and distended. This bulging, loose vein that we call "varicose" is simply a beaten-up and tired vein that we can see.

If you know your mother and grandmother suffered from varicose veins, there isn't much you can do. Ideally, you should spend most of your life in bed, flexing your legs in the air as often as you can, while the maid brings you tea. But this idyllic lady-of-leisure lifestyle is, fortunately or unfortunately, not an option for most people.

I've talked about mothers and daughters and ladies of leisure on purpose. Varicose veins are primarily a female problem. Some men are also born with deficient valves, but there are a few special events in a woman's life that really exacerbate the condition.

The worst of all is pregnancy. Until men get pregnant, women and their legs must bear all the burden. That includes astronomic estrogen levels which affect all the connective tissues. Ligaments get a little lax; the vein walls soften and become prone to distension and hydraulic damage.

Pregnancy also means a great mass of weight sitting on the pelvis. Pregnant women aren't carrying only the extra weight of a fetus: they must also bear the burden of the fetus's support system, the amniotic sac and other goodies which, combined, can weigh one and a half times as much as the fetus alone. This not only puts pressure on their legs, but also blocks the blood's way back to the heart by acting as a dam on the blood's upward flow.

There's not a lot you can do to prevent getting varicose veins. You can't very well change your genetics, and you probably want to live your life being up and about. Avoiding varicose veins is hardly a good reason to remain childless; and besides, you won't know until you are pregnant if the pregnancy will have that effect on you.

However, there are some things you can and should do if you see varicose veins developing. Support hose are a necessity, especially during a pregnancy. Whether you opt for the lightweight, cosmetically appealing variety for veins that aren't seriously distended yet, or go for the steel-belted radials that frankly look ugly, they do help. You may not want to enter any beauty pageants with them on, but they'll tide you over the rough times. Daily midday rests – lying flat, preferably with legs raised – during the pregnancy and for six weeks after, is time well invested.

Full-blown varicose veins can be a real annoyance. They can make your legs hurt when you stand. They can swell and be uncomfortable. They can even change the colour of your skin and cause ulcerations.

But don't sit down! The blood in your legs will just pool and you'll end up with a swamp. Walking is better than standing or sitting because it flexes your muscles. Lying down and elevating your legs will drain the swamp.

If your varicose veins cause you real problems, it may be time for dramatic solutions. Surgery for varicose veins is not a trivial procedure and should be considered only if you've carefully balanced your discomfort and lifestyle problems against the benefits of intervention. It means removing only the superficial veins which have become varicose, so it may not solve all your problems.

A slightly less serious medical treatment is injection. It is much less disabling in the short term than surgery. But it ain't pretty. If you're squeamish, you'd better turn the page.

The solution injected into the vein creates an intense inflammation which causes the blood to clot. You have to be treated immediately after the injection to make sure you don't wind up with a severe clotting in the vein. With proper care, this process will result in the actual closing of the vein. It is scarred shut and eventually vanishes.

Vein stripping or injections sound fairly extreme, but you should realize you are thoughtfully equipped with two complete systems of veins in your legs. There is a deep system in the muscles and a superficial system, the one you see under the skin. You can do with one set only, if need be. If the superficial system is scarred or removed, the inner veins will work just fine. They've probably long since taken over, anyway, if the superficial system has become varicose.

There aren't any nice things to say about varicose veins. They're one of the unhappy things our bodies do to us without so much as a by-your-leave. But if you suffer from them, they might serve one small purpose in the ongoing battle of the sexes. Men, as you know, always accuse women of not being able to read a road map. The next time you hear this tired sexist remark, point down to your calves and say you know it isn't true. Why, right there south of your knee is the road to Santa Fe.

THIS LITTLE PIGGY STAYED AT HOME

An ingrown toenail is not one of the world's sexy complaints, but if you're the person who is hobbling around in pain, it is pretty important. There is, however, a cure. You cut a V-shaped notch in the centre of the ailing nail.

Well, sometimes it works – and usually it doesn't. An ingrown toenail occurs when the corners of your toenail actually grow down into the flesh instead of riding up over it and coming out at the end of your toe the way they are supposed to. Instead of cutting the nail straight across or cutting it rounded at the front like a car's bumper, you cut it into the centre so that the corners are sticking out farther than the middle. When you look at it from above (as is so often the case with toes), it looks like a V. It shortens the central part of the nail so that your shoes can't push down on the top of your toenail and force the corners into the flesh.

But sometimes a V is not enough. There are variations on this theme which are actually better at keeping the pressure off the corners where the real trouble is. You can do this by filing the flat part thin in the centre. This allows the sides to ride up a bit as you walk and relieves the pressure. Or you can cut the corners on a bevel rather than leaving them sharply angled. With any luck, they'll grow over and out. All this can be quite creative. You could consider it toe-piary art.

Needless to say, for severe cases surgery is an option. It's painful and unpleasant, but it's like hitting your head against a brick wall: it feels so good when you stop.

Most people, quite rightly, have no interest in toenails until they hurt enough. They don't cut them properly to begin with, and they wear narrow shoes that might be quite fashionable but are death to toenails. Prevention is usually the best cure. That means a regular clipping straight across with a small notch at the centre and unglamorous footwear with a roomy toe box.

Toenails aren't ordinarily a family doctor's domain. When patients come in for a physical, they're usually concerned about the state of their more vital organs. So when I start talking about their toenails, they think I've lost my grip. But having been a sufferer myself, I have a minor fetish about the subject.

I happen to care about toenails, even painted ones. Call me crazy, but call me if they hurt.

JACK FROST NIPPING AT YOUR NOSE

I'm a skier, part of the minuscule segment of the population who actually likes snow. I like it a lot – but not well enough to rub it on my hands or face should I get frostbitten. I've heard that's what you're supposed to do. And apparently some folks actually believe this.

I'm always flabbergasted that this particular myth is still bandied about. It makes sense in a homeopathic sort of way: "treat cold with cold." But stop and think about it.

The one thing you can guarantee about snow is that it is below freezing. Now, if you're suffering from frostbite, a small portion of your skin is frozen. Why would you want to extend the area by rubbing all around it with snow? Rub your face or your toes with snow and you'll just take more heat out of the area surrounding the frostbite.

In addition, if your face is frostbitten, the skin is extremely fragile. And snow is crystalline with lots of tiny, sharp edges. Why would you want to rub your face with a million teensy razor blades and risk tearing it and damaging it even more?

Obviously you shouldn't plunge a frostbitten finger into a hot cup of tea. But heat, not more cold, is the answer. The trick is to warm the frostbite sloooooowly.

If I'm schussing down a hill in thirty-below temperatures and my face starts to tingle, I can take care of this simply enough by taking a mitt off, putting my hand over the area and letting my own body heat thaw the frostbite out. Of course, it would help enormously if I stop to do this – and if I put on a balaclava before I start downhill again.

That works for most minor frostbites. In the case of a major one, remember that it's not just the skin that is frozen – the underlying tissues are too, and the bone and blood structures may be also. It's important to warm everything from the inside out. Obviously you should come in from the cold as quickly as possible and warm your body all over so that it can pump heat out. When the frostbite thaws, you have to be able to supply blood to it because, if you don't, the area will use up all its own oxygen and could kill itself off.

You can identify frostbite by an absence of colour. If you're skiing with friends on a bitterly cold day, stop every so often to look at each other's faces. If you notice any white areas on cheeks or noses, from the size of a pinprick to the size of a dollar coin, even if the person isn't feeling any discomfort, you'll know the skin is frozen. If you must ski alone, it wouldn't be too crazy an idea to carry a small mirror in your pocket.

Fingers and toes may be white, too, if they're frostbitten, but more likely they'll be bright red; they're trying desperately to fight the cold by furiously pumping extra blood throughout. So stop and take care of them immediately. If you wait until they turn white, it may be too late.

Once you've been frozen and thawed out, don't go back out to freeze again. Fortunately most ski areas have accessible shelters. If you must go out again or you couldn't get indoors in the first place, cover the thawed-out area as best you can and don't expose it again until you can go inside once and for all.

Minor frostbite may leave you with a blister, exactly the same sort of thing you'd get from a minor burn. It will heal by itself. Major frostbite can be serious – it may kill off tissue in the area and even lead to gangrene. If you're badly frozen, get medical attention as soon as possible.

Frostbite is one of the least pleasant things in a winter wonderland. Once you've had it, you might find that area extremely sensitive to any cold. The sensitivity will fade over time, but some people swear it never goes away completely. A frostbitten finger may forever bother you each time you pick up a cold soft drink can. It's not the sort of memory most of us want to have of winter.

THE SOUND OF ONE KNUCKLE CRACKING

Don't you just cringe when you hear people crack their knuckles? It's an awful habit and, besides, it can cause arthritis. Or is that just a myth spread by those of us who hate the sound?

It's not a myth. Tell that to the knuckle crackers you know. There are several kinds. There are the pullers and there are the benders. The pullers are the people who grab the end of their digit and jerk it straight out with a clunk, one finger after the other. Then there are the benders, the people who either turn their hands backwards and push them out until they all sort of crack simultaneously, or the people who roll one hand inside the other and then bend it down and make a noise like crushing a bag full of marbles or walnuts. They are the ones who, sitting down at the piano, always add some of that ugly percussion before they start to play.

I don't know why people do it. I suppose it becomes a habit, like many other ticks or spasms we develop. It's also true that not everyone can do it. Some of us could crunch our fingers all we wanted and not get that satisfactory sound.

As an occasional party trick, cracking your knuckles isn't harmful. But it can be if indulged in on a regular basis over a long period of time. Most of us will suffer from wear-and-tear arthritis over the years. But knuckle crackers – the ones who hyper-extend and flex their finger joints – are absolutely sure to get it.

All of us have natural stops built into our joints. We can push them just so far and no farther. But knuckle crackers are constantly forcing their joints beyond the normal range of motion. Frequently mistreating the joints like this is bound to damage something. So if you have a natural tendency towards arthritis and you want to make it much worse, you just go ahead and crack those knuckles.

As for the rest of your body, cracking bits and pieces of it now and again probably won't do you any harm. Some people can get very satisfying clunks from their neck, back, hip, or knees. However, they don't do it thirty times a day, year after year after year, the way knuckle crackers do.

Once in a while, and probably not even on purpose, you get that little clunk. Some of these actually are good. If you get a clunk from your back or neck, it might relieve some discomfort you've got back there. Some clunks in other parts of your body might matter more than others, and that's the problem. If you've got a grind or a click or a clunk, usually you don't know whether it's good or bad. But as a general rule, the ones in your neck or back don't matter very much.

The ones that can matter are those in your knees. If your knees go crunch all the time, you should think about seeing a doctor. It might turn out to be an oddity of your body – but it might also indicate a condition that is completely preventable. A torn cartilage, for example, could be serious but is treatable. If the tear is between the surfaces of the joint, it could make a constant crunching sound. Or it could go off quite loudly, like the report of a small-bore rifle. This can be rather dramatic – especially if you're sitting in church. These are important sounds to pay attention to. If a torn cartilage is the cause, you should have the torn bit removed or else it will act like sand in the gears grinding up the joint surfaces over the years.

If the rest of you occasionally sounds like the Tin Man rattling down the Yellow Brick Road, I wouldn't lose too much sleep over it. You probably just need some oil.

TOUGH AS NAILS

Eat your lime Jell-o. It will make your fingernails grow long and strong." It's time to scratch the surface of another You-Are-What-You-Eat myth.

Gelatin doesn't make your fingernails grow long and strong. The idea that it does is a classic jump in logic. Nails, you see, are almost pure protein. So is gelatin. Somewhere along the line, some bright soul figured out that if your nails are brittle and cracking, they probably are protein deficient. Enter Jell-o – lime or cherry or orange, whichever you prefer.

But protein, when it's swallowed, doesn't know where it is supposed to go. A protein molecule is a very long molecule of coupled amino acids, hooked head to tail, end to end, ready to be of service in our general make-up.

We digest protein by cracking off one amino acid at a time so that it can be absorbed by our system. But once it's in there, it has no particular destination. It's distributed by our metabolic machinery. Protein is quite promiscuous: it goes where it's needed and, if it's not needed, it turns into sugar. That's why protein can provide calories.

I didn't find out about this myth until quite late in life. I always thought the idea was to keep your nails short so that the dirt couldn't hide in them. But when I was first married, my wife used to complain about her nails, which used to crack and split – and do to this day. I also discovered she had a gelatin habit.

When she explained it all to me, I started to notice that, indeed, gelatin is a very commonly advertised nostrum for this problem. There were ads in glossy magazines recommending gelatin powder in your coffee (which leaves a scummy mess at the bottom of your cup), and gelatin capsules and all sorts of things. It sounds delightfully simple as a solution – but it doesn't work!

The only real solution I can think of is artificial nails. They work quite wonderfully because they are made long and strong and they stay put until you decide to take them off.

If your own nails aren't made long and strong, there really isn't anything you can do about it. You can't change their structure. They are formed in the nail bed in layers. If some of those layers don't adhere properly as they're being put down, the nails that grow will be brittle and crack easily with the slightest stress.

This natural state of affairs can be made worse by environmental factors. Teachers rightly complain about handling chalk dust all the time because it makes their hands extremely dry and their nails don't form properly. Dryness in general isn't conducive to healthy nail growth; this is the reason so many people notice their nails break more easily in the winter. But the basic underlying problem is one of genetics.

Your genetic codes will not only determine whether your nails grow long and hard or soft and brittle but also whether they will grow full of little ridges and pits. People who have all twenty nails like that have probably always had them that way.

An occasional ridge or pit could be the aftermath of a disease. Psoriasis, especially, will show up in your fingertips, sometimes quite dramatically in grotesque malformations. We also know that a recurrent illness, such as a serious flu, will affect the nails that grow out after your bout. But the damage is temporary – you can actually watch a ridge grow out progressively along the nail over a period of months.

An acute, traumatic injury of a limb, such as a broken leg, can also have an impact on the way the toenails grow. But it won't affect your fingernails. A broken arm might, but then your toenails would be okay.

Minor injuries to the nail itself will show up as small, white spots. The nail bed actually goes into our skin about two millimetres below our nails. If we hit that area while a nail is forming, even so slightly that we don't notice it, it might show up as a white spot that takes a few months to grow out. It's sort of like the rings on a tree which are a record of what's happened to the tree as it grew.

As for the white half-moons most people have, they are perfectly normal at any size and no indication of health. Usually, the deepest moon is on the thumb, and the moons get less visible as you go across the hand to the pinkie. I've never considered them to be signs of either beauty or ugliness – they just happen.

Your nails, like your hair, may be affected by diet. An extreme protein or vitamin deficiency will result in poorly formed nails. But if you are suffering from either of those, the appearance of your nails is the least of your problems.

What you do to your nails won't bother them. Nails are insensate, quite dead from the time they are formed. They are simply a pile of protein being pushed out by the protein building up behind. But you can make a difference to the way they look by taking care of them.

Polish is not a bad idea because it penetrates into the nails ever so slightly and does have a hardening effect. It's the same effect as varnishing wood.

The way you cut your nails can also make a difference. Those small end-clippers are fine for most people, but if you are the type whose nails tend to split, clipping will increase that tendency. The cut formed by an end clipper can be the initial cleavage plane down the nail. Filing is definitely the better way for splitters.

Don't throw away those end clippers, though. They are great for pruning your cat's claws. And, while you're at it, feed him the lime Jell-o.

TOADYING TO WARTS

When I was a kid, like all little boys I thought frogs and toads were pretty terrific. It wasn't till later that I discovered all those toads I'd been keeping in my pockets were supposed to have covered my hands in warts. Talk about a bad reputation!

Looking at a toad it's easy to see where this particular myth originated. Toads are covered with warty-looking bumps. Since we know warts are infectious, it's not a far-fetched leap-frog of the imagination to assume the toad's warts can spread to your hand. Yet somehow people don't seem to worry about catching "eyes" from handling a potato. I guess it's because most of us wouldn't mind an extra set of eyes in odd places, but nobody I know has ever wished for warts.

Warts are caused by a virus, a particular class of virus which is capable of causing unusual growths in the epidermis, your skin. The result is a kind of tumour – a benign tumour, but a tumour nonetheless.

The virus causes a hyperactive growth of the germinal, or formative, layer of your skin. It causes your cells to heap up in swirls and great strands that you can see under the microscope. It all looks rather abnormal and, indeed, it is. It also causes the growth of blood vessels to support this new mass of tissue. This explains why, when you take a wart off, it bleeds and also why the wart appears to contain black specks – the blood vessels often develop a little thrombosis, a clot, which becomes solid and turns black.

Like all viruses, the one that causes warts can be contagious. Kids seem to pass them to each other like baseball cards. It can also rage through a family, hitting Mom and Dad as well as brothers and sisters. But it's not as highly contagious as, say, chicken pox, which shows no mercy. Not everyone seems to be hospitable to the wart virus. We don't really know why some people pick it up in a flash and others seem to be immune.

One thing we do know is that anxiety has nothing to do with it. A lot of diseases and conditions are blamed on "nerves," but there is no empirical evidence that stress makes a person susceptible to warts.

As for treatments, if you consult ten doctors, you will probably find ten ways of getting rid of the warts. Sometimes the warts do fall off by themselves – I like it when that happens because I usually get the credit. It's the old medicine man approach.

The truth is, warts can be extremely nasty to treat. When I am confronted with a case, I have no guarantee that what worked perfectly with the last person will work at all with the next one. I keep wondering what I've done wrong. Sometimes warts just get better by themselves. Sometimes warts won't get better no matter what you do. And sometimes, if you're lucky, your treatment works.

Most doctors rely on widely available, over-the-counter preparations like Duofill and Compound W. They work very well for some people – but for others, you may as well apply plain old tap water.

Then there are more rigorous preparations which are more destructive than the drugstore remedies. These have to be prescribed by a doctor because they're quite toxic. Surgery is also an option, usually cauterization, which involves burning the area with a needle so that the natural healing process works on everything in its path. There are immune treatments which are relatively expensive and sometimes tremendously effective but sometimes disastrous. Cryotherapy, with liquid nitrogen, is an uncomfortable but effective treatment for many types of warts.

I could go on, but I think you're getting the idea. There are a whole host of treatments, but not one of them is perfect. A perfect treatment would be easy to apply, cheap, non-toxic, and effective every time. There isn't a single wart treatment that fills the bill.

Warts are not a neglected field. If you read the medical literature, you'll see that there is considerable research under way. The drug companies certainly would love to find a magic bullet – it would help a lot of people and, not coincidentally, make a lot of money. But we aren't there yet. Not many people still believe in the old toad-wart connection. After all, how many toads do most people run into downtown in a major city? I'm not even sure that the toads believe it any more. But they've still got the warts.

It's in the
BLOOD

RUDOLF THE RED-NOSED DRUNK

Did Rudolf the Reindeer have a drinking habit? The image we have, thanks especially to old W.C. Fields movies, is that someone with a red, bulbous nose is a heavy imbiber.

Some people who never touch a drop can get a nose like that. But when you see someone with a bright red schnoz walk into a bar, you're right to speculate.

Heavy drinkers frequently have red faces, not just noses, all the time. It's not embarrassment. Even modest amounts of alcohol can cause a flush. If your face is flushed all the time, eventually the redness doesn't go away. Chronic imbibing may dilate the blood vessels until they are no longer capable of constricting.

There is another possible explanation. Excessive alcohol intake can cause liver damage. When your liver packs it in, your ability to metabolize estrogen is severely impaired and your estrogen levels go up. That may not be disastrous for women whose bodies are used to dealing with estrogen fluctuations. But for men there are a few interesting side-effects. One of the more common is a vessel malformation called a spider nevus.

This consists of a central feeder vessel, the body of the spider, and small, dilated capillaries, the spider's legs. If you push down on the centre, the legs blanch because their blood supply has been cut off. If you see someone with six or seven spiders on his face, you had better ask about his drinking habits.

An enlarged nose is usually evident in people over fifty. But the spider nevi can show up at any age – I've seen them in a twenty-five year old with alcoholic cirrhosis.

The worst cases of a red, bulbous nose are called "rhinophyma." This sounds like a vacation resort in Italy, but once you go there, you never come back. Plastic surgery may work for some. It reduces the size of the nose but still leaves the red, rough skin.

If you have a Rudolf nose, remember that the large, dilated blood vessels can bleed briskly if they're punctured, so stay out of bar room brawls. But other than that, rhinophyma doesn't pose any dangers – aside from social stigma.

NOT FOR THE FAINT OF HEART

The heroine's name is Emily. She's a fragile flower, perhaps an antebellum Southern beauty standing in the living room of a grand old house. The butler hands her a letter. She reads it; she's overcome; she faints. How many times have you watched this scene in a movie or a play?

I've seen it on stage or on the screen hundreds of times. But never in real life. People do faint at the sight of gore. But never at unpleasant news.

The key to this puzzle is that the swooners are always female. If we saw a play in which a man swooned, we'd know right away that he's some sort of wimp. It's Not Done.

All this goes back to Victorian England where the better class of people were convinced that women couldn't cope. It was culturally acceptable for a woman to faint in the case of a severe shock. She certainly couldn't scream in terror or start throwing the philodendrons, but swooning was "cool."

If you've experienced a tremendous emotional shock such as the death of a loved one, or an extremely scary situation such as nearly being run down by a Mack truck, you know that afterwards you can feel totally befuddled for a few minutes or a few hours. Your brain seems to click off: you're incapable of clear thought and feel tremulous as if you're going to faint. You don't usually faint, but being on the brink like that makes you think all those stage histrionics are plausible.

What is a faint, anyway? As long as you're alive, you can be in one of two states: awake or not awake. If you have inadequate blood flow to your brain, your brain cannot keep you awake. Perhaps you've seen a person who has been lying down suddenly get up to answer the telephone. He is not emotionally upset, but you'd think he was about to keel over.

What happened is that the veins in his legs filled up with blood as he stood up. His blood, literally, fell to the bottom of his body and did not come back up fast enough. His heart didn't have enough blood to pump up to the brain and he could have sunk like a stone any minute.

The most serious faints occur with a cardiac arrest. The faint may be the first visible sign that you're in dire straits. It also may be the last thing you do! Ordinarily, fainting is self-correcting. Once you're horizontal, the proper flow of blood is restored. But it behoves us all to check a fainting person to see if he or she has suffered a heart attack. And, if we've all taken our CPR courses (I strongly recommend them), we all know how to check for cardiac arrest. The three seconds it takes could save a life.

The garden variety faint, as I've said, is due to an inadequate return of blood from the veins in our legs. You've all seen TV news footage of a young soldier in a wool uniform standing out in the hot sun while his platoon is inspected by a visiting dignitary. Suddenly he keels over in the middle of the parade square, and the Queen or the President or whoever tries not to notice.

This happens because the soldier was standing far too still. You need to keep your leg muscles moving to keep the blood flowing up the veins back to the heart. But if the muscles are flaccid because you're standing at attention and if, in addition, it's hot and all your blood vessels are dilated, your blood pools below, doesn't go back up properly, your heart doesn't pump the blood to the brain and – STRIKE! – you go over like a bowling pin. Then, blood flows to your heart, cardiac output goes up, you wake up. Of course, you're embarrassed and your nose is broken. And you're probably in the brig for having disgraced the regiment.

The next time you watch the troops lined up for inspection, take a close look. You will notice that most of the soldiers are rocking back and forth, and from side to side, to keep their blood flowing. To really see it, you'd have to stand at the end of the line and watch their noses – not an easy task for a civilian during inspection. And certainly not recommended if you suffer from seasickness.

Apart from troops in formation and Victorian ladies, pregnant women are especially prone (no pun intended) to fainting. Pregnancy causes a "vasamotor instability," or an inappropriate dilation of the blood vessels. A woman who has never fainted before in her life can be the third person in a slow-moving line at the bank and down she goes, in full view of everyone. And it's not just a way of jumping the queue.

One of the silliest things people do when they see someone about to faint is to say, "Why don't you sit down in this chair?" Sitting down keeps most of the body vertical. What you should do is lie her right down wherever she is. People will often resist, especially in a bank when the only time you're usually asked to lie on the floor is during a hold-up.

But that's exactly what you should do. Convince her to give in to the impulse to lie down. If possible, elevate her heels onto your knees. She'll get a sudden transfusion of blood from the extremities into the heart and – Good morning!

Although I have never fainted at the sight of blood, fainting's not all that uncommon in medical school. When I was a student, a friend and I were watching a particularly tricky bit of cardiovascular surgery. The patient's entire abdomen was opened up, and all the abdominal contents had been set to one side. We all could see a huge aneurysm at the back of the abdomen.

The surgeon deftly removed it and put a graft nicely in place. Now came the moment of truth: would the graft hold? He asked that the upper clamp be released. The patient's first heartbeat came down like a water hammer and split the bottom of the graft wide open. Before the clamp could be put back in place, blood spurted up and into the room like water from a punctured garden hose.

A jet of blood hit my friend and washed right across his masked face and his glasses. It may have been a combination of having stood absolutely rooted in one place and being sprayed by the sudden gore. But down he went. Not straight down, mind you – he fell forward, right across the patient. You might say he fell into the operation.

He had not scrubbed, neither was he gowned. The flabbergasted surgeon quickly grabbed him by the shoulders, picked him up, and dropped him unceremoniously on the floor. But now the wound was contaminated, the surgeon was contaminated, the assistant was contaminated, the instruments were contaminated, everything was contaminated.

I dragged my friend by the heels out of the operating room into the hallway. The nurses and the surgeons tried to regown and redrape, but of course they could never undo what had been done. The surgeon finished off as best he could. They put the patient back together and over the next few weeks, they all held their breath and crossed their fingers waiting for the patient's wound to become an infected mess.

Except nothing happened. Nothing. So either we got very lucky that day or the germ theory of disease is a lie. I'm still not too sure which.

THE KISSING DISEASE

W hen you were a kid, did you think mononucleosis was "sexy"? The idea was that you caught mono by kissing. It was as close as we came, in those innocent days, to knowing about a social disease.

But months of bed rest seemed a high price to pay for a kiss. That's what we thought the cure was. It seems we were wrong on all counts.

Mononucleosis has long been shrouded in myth and mystery. It's only in the last two decades that research has lifted the veil. Mono is a glandular fever caused by a virus. Its name comes from the fact that the disease's presence is indicated by an increase in leukocytes, or white blood cells, with only one nucleus.

Like many other diseases, mononucleosis is spread by poverty – or, rather, by the crowded living conditions that characterize poverty. But you don't have to be poor to catch it. Take a nice, middle-class kid who has lived all his life in his own room in his own home. He's gone to the local school which, being in a good neighbourhood, isn't overcrowded. Then he goes to college.

All of a sudden, he's sharing a space with forty other kids, all living in each other's pockets. And he contracts mono. Then the others get it. And on it goes, back and forth through the whole lot of them.

His parents don't know what's going on. But they do know he's off on his own for the first time. And probably necking with some girl. So "kissing" must be the culprit. It can't be as simple as living in a crowded space. I'm surprised the disease isn't associated with letter sweaters or something else equally ridiculous.

It has only been in the last few years that we've realized that anyone can get mono and that most people do, but don't know it. Children from large families often contract the disease at the age of seven or eight, when it is frequently misdiagnosed as the flu. Those of us raised in less crowded conditions are more likely to avoid mono until later in life.

Kissing could do it. It is, after all, a viral infection and viruses are transmitted from person to person by contact. But when you live in close quarters with other people, there are many ways of spreading a virus – hand to hand, mouth to hand, hand to object, object to hand, and so on.

Most people don't even know that they have it. Mono can be a fairly trivial disease, especially in the very young. Its symptoms are a fever and swollen glands. So if a five-year-old is slightly off-colour, her parents keep her home for a few days and then send her back to school. They chalk it up to a flu or something. They aren't aware that she had mono.

Even doctors are confused by it. An eighteen-year-old kid comes home from college with a terribly sore throat and his parents take him to the doctor. Both the parents and the doctor believe he has strep throat. His throat is red, he looks sick, he's running a fever, he has a slight rash and feels downright awful. So the doctor takes a culture and starts him on antibiotics right away because there's no point wasting time waiting for the lab results to come back.

Two days later, the patient is no better and the lab report comes back negative. So it's back to the doctor for a rethink. It happens all the time.

By now the mystery is about to be cleared up. Other symptoms are showing up. His rash is worse; his lymph glands are swollen. His spleen is so enlarged you can feel it through the abdomen.

Mono can have some rare but significant complications that range from muscle disorders, to neurological disorders, to disorders of the liver. It can be a very complex disease. Fortunately, most of the time it isn't. Its primary complication seems to be that it's an illness which is hard to diagnose.

In fact, that may be why people assume the cure is prolonged bed rest. Prolonged bed rest is a historic curiosity, originated by doctors and propagated by much repeating. A few days in bed may be warranted and not over extending yourself until you feel well is just common sense.

However most people who have mono don't feel all that fatigued. But six months of rest is certainly not mandatory. Nor is even one month. If you're capable of going out and doing things, you should be active. Lounging about all day is probably counter-productive.

Mono is contagious only the first few days that the symptoms appear. My advice is this: if you're feeling unwell, stay away from people. When you feel well enough, away you go. But it might be a good idea to save the kissing until you're really on top of the world again.

SWEETS FOR THE SWEET

There are many reasons to think twice before indulging in that second helping of pecan pie. But one of them is not that eating too much sugar could lead to diabetes.

This is a pernicious myth because it blames the victims for a disease they didn't create for themselves. Diabetes is a serious enough condition without adding guilt to it.

I don't deny there is a considerable connection between sugar and diabetes. But when someone is diagnosed as a diabetic, it's too easy to look back and say, "Ah, yes. I've certainly seen him eating chocolates or putting an extra spoon of sugar in his tea. That must be what caused it." The truth is that we all indulge on occasion, but we don't all get diabetes. I'm willing to bet there isn't a single one of us who doesn't deserve to be rapped on the knuckles for the dark days when we pigged out on sugar.

Diabetes is largely a genetic problem. If it's not in your family's history, chances are good you'll never get it. If any of your relatives had it, your chances go up according to how closely related you are. It also depends on how severe their diabetes is. If both your parents contracted it when they were seventy-three when everything else was wearing out, that's not a strong prognostic sign as far as you're concerned. But if they both had it as children, your chances become astronomically high.

The word "diabetes" is misleading because there are two different diseases with the same name. Medically speaking, the proper nomenclature is Type 1 and Type 2. But I find that confusing and hard to remember. The more common terms "juvenile diabetes" and "adult onset diabetes" are descriptive and correct. The two conditions are different from each other, but they share the problem of an error in sugar metabolism. It's easy to see why they are so often linked together.

Adult onset diabetes, as its name suggests, doesn't show up until a person is usually well into his or her adult years. Most people who get it are into their forties or fifties or even older. It appears quite insidiously and may have been present for more than a year before the person became aware of it or suffered any of its manifestations.

It's a common misconception that adult onset diabetes is a disease of insulin deficiency. Not so. Adult onset diabetics, in fact, probably have more insulin in their blood than non-diabetics. They are capable of making more insulin. But the problem is that their cells become insulin-resistant – they develop insulin antibodies so that what they make becomes ineffectual. We do treat it with insulin. But it's a matter of topping up, giving extra insulin to overcome the body's resistance to it.

Juvenile diabetes, on the other hand, is truly an insulin-deficient disease. Insulin is made in the pancreas, in the islets of Langerhans, which are scattered throughout the pancreas like salt and pepper. They are hormones; they dump their product right into the blood stream.

The islets contain beta cells, the cells which actually manufacture the insulin. If you look at the pancreas of a juvenile diabetic, you will see that there are no beta cells there at all. An adult onset diabetic, on the other hand, has tons of beta cells which are very active.

Juvenile diabetes is classed as an "auto-immune" disease. Your own immune system forgets that a part of you is you. It thinks that some parts of you are actually The Enemy and proceeds to kill them off. It's like troops getting confused in battle and shooting at their own by mistake. The result in a juvenile diabetic is that he loses all ability to make his own insulin.

It's a fragile existence. The patient eats some sugar and the sugar in his blood rockets up. He takes some insulin and the sugar plummets down. There is no cushioning effect as there is with adult onset diabetes where the patient's own insulin can carry some of the load.

Obviously, then, the treatment of the two diseases is different. You can control adult onset diabetes with diet alone. Losing weight decreases the size of the patient's fat cells, which in turn decreases the number of insulin molecules required. Oral medications can stimulate further production of insulin by the pancreas. Insulin injections are rarely needed.

For juvenile diabetes, none of this works. Insulin is needed immediately. The patient tends to be brittle, and her insulin levels have to be balanced against the sugar at all times. It's not that she fails to look after herself. It's that the sugar levels go up and down extremely and her body refuses to regulate them.

Yet we tend to be very harsh toward diabetics, accusing them of self-indulgence and self-neglect. But it's too convenient to blame people for their own misfortunes. Some poor juvenile diabetic might be doing her best to look after herself and to control her sugar intake, her insulin adjustment, her lifestyle – and she still suffers terribly from the disease. I think it's very unfair to a person like that to claim she "caught" it from eating too many chocolates.

A SHOT IN THE ARM

If you step on a rusty nail, what do you get? Do you just get a cut foot? No, there is tetanus in dem der rusty nails. You'd better trundle off to the nearest emergency room or your family doctor to have a tetanus shot right away.

Tetanus is a nasty disease. It has a high mortality rate. But it's entirely preventable. If you get your tetanus immunization, I'll guarantee you won't get tetanus. And you don't need a shot every time you have a cut. After your primary immunization series, a booster will keep your immunization up for five years, perhaps even ten.

Tetanus is caused by bacteria, and we can catch it from all sorts of places. But we tend to always associate tetanus with puncture wounds, particularly those involving jagged metal.

The association is accurate as far as it goes. The bacteria that cause tetanus are everywhere, especially in soil. So a dirty wound is most likely to cause it. Sharp metal objects usually create puncture wounds. People think rust and dirt are the same thing – they are not – but it is true that they are often found together. You can cut yourself with something that looks relatively clean and still get tetanus.

The important thing is not what you cut yourself on, but how you cut yourself. A straight cut might not give you any problems, but torn, gouged, or crushed flesh is a good breeding ground for the infection.

If you have a shot every five years, you're safe. In the case of an injury that occurs during that five-year interval, I wouldn't bother about shots. The question is, how do you remember to keep your immunization up? I flag the date from the date of my graduation from medical school. Every five years, on that anniversary, I get a shot. What a way to celebrate!

The first time I decided to do this, I had been in practice for about four years. After happily jabbing a lot of people that particular day, I decided it was time to take a dose of my own medicine. So just before closing time, I went to the fridge and got out a tetanus-polio vaccine vial (you really should always take them together). I filled up the syringe and was just about to plunge it into my upper arm when ... my hand froze. It stayed stuck just above my shoulder and wouldn't budge. Nothing could make me give myself that needle.

I was really angry with myself for having nonchalantly pricked so many other people and finding out I couldn't inject myself. I was so annoyed that when my secretary (who has no medical training whatsoever) walked by, I handed her the needle and said, "Shove it in right there." She did. And that's how I got my tetanus shot.

If you haven't kept your immunizations up and step on a rusty nail, you probably do need a shot. But there's no hurry. The bacteria take days to grow in the flesh before you have a toxic effect: you don't have to rush right off and have your shot within hours. If I had an injury and it wasn't convenient for me to get to the doctor's till the next day, I'd wait until then knowing I was safe.

In the meantime, it's wise to cleanse the wound. But I wouldn't count on iodine or any other ointment to protect me against the tetanus.

Chances are you have been immunized but may simply not remember. It's unusual for anyone these days not to have received at least a primary immunization. There are a few religious groups who will not accept immunization of any kind. But anybody who has been in, for example, the armed services or who held down certain kinds of jobs will have received the shots automatically somewhere along the line.

For the occasional adult who never has, this can be a problem. He doesn't have a primary immunity and has to "borrow" it from someone else by getting that person's globulin by injection. He has to go through the same series of shots that a baby goes through. That's five in all. The doctor will affirm that the shots are painless because they are done with a small-bore needle which causes very little reaction. It certainly doesn't cause a swollen arm or anything.

But still, five needles are five needles — when one every five years could have done.

A Case of
NERVES

HIGH TENSION WIRED

You gotta cool down. You gotta relax. Take it sloooow, man. Take it easy. If you don't, your veins are gonna blow.

Well, I've got some news for you. You can be cool as a cucumber and still suffer from hypertension. Resolving your emotional problems is not going to lower your blood pressure. I wish it were that simple, but medical reality has a way of making mincemeat of common sense.

The problem is the word "hypertension" itself. Just look at it: it's made up of "hyper" and "tension." If that doesn't sound wired, I don't know what does.

In ordinary, everyday language, hypertension is very descriptive. It suggests a state of excitability, extreme agitation, perhaps even anger. You think that someone suffering from "hypertension" must be up on the ceiling, or at least off the wall. But in a scientific sense, "hypertension" just means high blood pressure. Doctors, unfortunately, tend to be sloppy in their use of language. They'll use the word both in its ordinary sense and in its medical sense. No wonder their patients get confused.

It is true that if you are emotional, angry, or frightened, your blood pressure shoots up – temporarily. When you're walking across the street and a car screeches to a horn-blowing halt with its bumper resting against your knee, your blood pressure can shoot up thirty points and stay there for two hours.

Sometimes simply visiting your physician to have your blood pressure tested may drive it up. It's a real problem for both doctor and patient because the reading taken during that particular visit will not be a true reflection of your normal blood pressure. In such cases, I loan out a stethoscope and a pressure cuff to the patient. I ask the patient's spouse or a friend to come into the office to learn how the equipment works. Then I send them both away and ask them to keep a record over a period of a week or so. The patient's blood pressure should ideally be checked first thing in the morning, after experiencing stress, during relaxation, and so on. The record, often at variance with what I found during the office visit, gives me a good idea of what sort of blood pressure the patient has normally.

Statistically, some emotional people have high blood pressure and some calm folks have it too. On the other hand, some spaced-out dudes have perfectly normal blood pressure and some cool cukes really are cool.

If it's not your emotions, then what does cause hypertension in the medical sense? It could be the symptom of an underlying disease. Temporarily lowering the person's blood pressure isn't going to solve the real problem. If you find and treat the disease, the hypertension will probably take care of itself. In the majority of cases, however, we just don't know what causes high blood pressure. The word we use to describe this category of hypertension is "idiopathic." "Idio" means unknown, and "pathic" means disease. It is an unknown disease. I think it really means we're idiots not to know.

There is a lot of research under way and, fortunately, as time goes on, more and more types of hypertension are separated out of the great pack of idiopathics and put into the "we know" class of disease.

There are also some myths about the treatment of hypertension. We know that lots of salt is not good, but if you eliminate it, will it help? You should always be prudent in your salt consumption whether you have hypertension or not, but you can't eliminate it. That's a physical impossibility. In fact, eliminating it would be lethal. Our bodies need some salt to function properly.

If you're a salt freak and gorge on salty things, there is certainly some room for improvement. But if you follow a normal, rounded diet, it would be difficult to decrease your salt intake dramatically. I became acutely aware of what I was doing to my patients when I asked them to cut down on their salt. One year, at our medical staff rounds held at lunch time, we tried a different therapeutic diet once a week. The absolute worst was the low-salt. The food looked like food, but it tasted like cardboard. So I know it takes tremendous self-discipline to go on a stringent low-salt diet. Even if you do, there's no promise this will have a positive effect.

People also believe high blood pressure is related to being overweight. Once in a while, that's true, but you can suffer from hypertension without being overweight. I know of people who have worked very hard to lower their weight only to discover that their blood pressure is still too high.

Some people try yoga or meditation to relieve their hypertension. These relaxation techniques may indeed cause a normal person's blood pressure to drop slightly. But they don't have a long-term therapeutic effect. Nor does exercising a lot or "blowing off steam." Because these attempts are beneficial to the body as a whole, I wouldn't discourage anyone from trying them but don't expect your blood pressure to decrease as a result.

I know you're beginning to wonder: does *anything* relieve hypertension? All the methods I have mentioned do have a cumulative effect that's positive. But how much can you realistically change a person's lifestyle? If I asked you to make the four or five changes I've just described, would you be able to stick with all of them? It's worth trying, but from my experience, I know it's asking a lot.

For significant cases of hypertension, drugs can be beneficial. We do know that lowering the blood pressure reverses the damage done and has a dramatic effect in decreasing incidents of heart attacks and stroke. But remember that any drug can have side-effects and nowhere is this more true than with hypertensive drugs. Your doctor should start you off on mild ones and be prepared to juggle and jiggle to find the right medication at the right dose for you.

There is good news for sufferers of hypertension. It can be controlled through a combination of lifestyle changes and drugs where necessary. Awareness and control have gone a long way in combatting the diseases that result from hypertension. So stay cool.

CAN'T STOMACH THE PAIN

All that stress and tension! It's eating my stomach away. It's giving me an ulcer. But at least I know what to do about it: I can drink lots of milk to coat my stomach. There, now I can relax."

The hardest myths to dispel are those started by doctors. Doctors have used milk for years to treat ulcers. It's not a bad treatment from time to time but it doesn't prevent the condition. Drinking milk on a regular basis is no guarantee that you'll never get ulcers, nor is drinking it now for an ulcer any guarantee that you won't get one again.

The kind of job you do and the amount of stress you feel have little to do with your chances of getting an ulcer. One study was done on floor traders in the stock exchange. Talk about a high-pressure job! The study found that floor traders actually have a lower ulcer rate than many other more sedentary executives. I have had many patients with low-tension jobs and nasty ulcers. There is no correlation between stress and ulcers. It seems anyone can get them.

We're not sure what causes ulcers. All the research so far has failed to find that one causative agent. And once again, when we don't know, "stress" or "nerves" takes the rap. After all you can't disprove it. But we do know certain simple things.

Most people use the term "stomach ulcers," but the majority of ulcers appear in the duodenum, the first part of the small bowel after the stomach.

The stomach contains hydrochloric acid, a very powerful acid indeed. It also produces enzymes and other strong chemicals which it needs to digest protein. The stomach itself is built to be resistant to all this, but the duodenum isn't. However, even the stomach sometimes can't take the pace.

The last straw could be anything. It could be alcohol. Or Aspirin. Hot foods may be to blame. There seems to be a connection with your eating habits. Floor traders, for example, are notorious for eating very irregularly. They eat a mouthful now and a mouthful then, and a mouthful again between deals. They may be producing less acid in short spurts and that may protect them.

Some people may not even know they have an ulcer because they don't feel any symptoms. These ulcers are called "silent ulcers." But it's far more common, when you have an ulcer, to experience pain. The pain usually occurs about half an hour after a meal. Food in the stomach acts as a buffer. The same is true of a glass of milk.

It takes only twenty or thirty minutes for your stomach to empty and be left unbuffered again, but the acid continues to be produced and that's when you feel the irritation.

People describe the pain differently. Sometimes it's sharp, like a knife twisting in the abdomen. Sometimes it's a dull, aching pain, and sometimes it can feel like cramps. But usually it's constant, an irritation in the stomach that may reach all the way through to your back, right between the shoulder blades. Some people get the pain most severely at night, waking up at four a.m. with intense discomfort. Any pain at any time is a good sign that you need to see a doctor.

You can't really prevent an ulcer by quitting your job at the ad agency and moving to Montana. It's also not true that "holding things in" will cause one. So if you've been yelling at people all these years to "let it out," you can stop now. You can also begin to moderate your alcohol intake and substitute acetaminophen for Aspirin. But even that may not help if you're susceptible to the condition.

Once you've got an ulcer, you have to be careful in your dietary habits. Keep off the booze and start long-term antacid therapy. Ordinary over-the-counter antacids which act as neutralizers are good, but there are newer and more effective medications that can actually turn off the acid production. Both can help in an acute case and sometimes prevent a recurrence.

The pain of an ulcer is bad enough but, unfortunately, the condition can get worse. If an ulcer, even a silent ulcer, perforates, it can cause blinding pain. It's a catastrophe that can be treated only in an operating room. A bleeding ulcer can be equally severe – it can cause anemia or shock. Fortunately it can usually be treated without surgery, but it's still a serious threat.

There is a fascinating new theory that ulcers are actually caused by bacteria. Research is not yet conclusive, but, should it prove to be true, the news for ulcer sufferers is good. Most bacteria can be effectively treated with antibiotics.

An ulcer isn't created by stress. But it can create great stress. Don't mistake the symptom for the cause.

TROUBLE IN TOTLAND

Everyone has encountered a child who can't sit still for more than a minute. We used to say he was "full of beans." We used to say other things, too, but this book is meant for the whole family. Now we call him "hyperactive." It sounds official and technical; it gives a certain kind of behaviour the status of a syndrome.

I think the term has come to be used too loosely. Not every overactive child is necessarily hyperactive. It's time to make a distinction between a child who simply has oodles of energy and a child who has something wrong with him. Just because yours is driving you crazy doesn't mean he's medically amiss.

The attraction of a term like "hyperactive" can lull you into false logic: if it's a "disease" there must be a "cure." But a parent's idea of hyperactivity is very rarely objective. Behaviour can be influenced by such simple factors as the time of day or the amount of time you've spent with the child.

A child is truly hyperactive when his level of activity is counter-productive: when it interferes with his ability to learn at school or his ability to get along with his family. A mere discipline problem is not hyperactivity.

I'm not convinced we really know what causes this condition. Theories abound. Some people, even some doctors believe sugar is the culprit. Others blame artificial dyes or additives in food. There is some evidence for all these beliefs, but there is just as much evidence against them. The problem is that, on this issue, people become True Believers and it's hard to shake their faith.

Putting these theories into practice can be difficult. You can try to eliminate all foods which contain artificial anything, but that means monitoring your child constantly, an impossibility if you take him to the zoo or a birthday party or any situation that is beyond your control. There's no proof this will work, but I'm all in favour of a healthy diet and don't want to discourage anyone from trying it.

Another option is family therapy. Counselling can help you, the parent, cope with some of your child's overactive or hyperactive behaviour patterns. This is really important because often parents, faced with a child with a destructive pattern of behaviour, unknowingly can develop some equally destructive patterns of their own. Needless to say, this only makes the situation worse.

There are drugs for hyperactivity, but I approach them with extreme caution. They are absolutely a last resort. I would never start a child on drug therapy without a second opinion, preferably of an expert in the field. It's a major step and should not be undertaken without long and careful consideration.

If you use drugs appropriately, they can make a significant difference. The effects on a child who was unable to function at school or at home can be dramatic. He becomes "normal" – productive at school and endurable at home.

Fortunately, a child who has been diagnosed as hyperactive will often outgrow the condition, whether or not he has been treated with medication. Maturity may be the best medicine. If your child has been on drugs, you should look forward to getting him off them. I recommend therapeutic trial periods without drugs from time to time to see if he's succeeding on his own. If he's been on drugs for six months, stop the treatment for a while. If he's all right without them, why start up again?

The best time to experiment is a summer vacation. Let him go a bit nuts outside where he can run and play. Give him a drug holiday. This is beneficial and should be done regularly.

You may have noticed that throughout this section I have referred to the hyperactive child as "he." I'm not relying on old-fashioned grammar; I am trying to reflect reality. The fact is that hyperactive kids are invariably little boys. I personally have never met a little girl who was labelled hyperactive. We don't know why this condition is predominantly male because we don't know what causes it. If we understood why it is gender-linked, we might understand where it comes from.

For now, anyway, it's just another reason for little girls to feel superior.

Bodies in
MOTION

ROCKING THE BOAT

A h! There's nothing like the open seas to clear the senses. Unless, of course, you happen to get seasick. And everyone knows that landlubbers are more prone to seasickness than sailors.

Tell that one to Lord Nelson. Old Horatio, admiral of the fleet and all, was constantly seasick. He had a wretched time of it all the way to Trafalgar. It's a good thing he won the battle, or the trip wouldn't have been worth his while.

Think about it: if you get seasick are you likely to want to become a sailor? This myth is the result of natural selection. If you go out on a boat for the first time and get violently ill, are you going to make this a career choice? No – you'll check the want ads for the land-based professions. Sailors don't get as seasick as landlubbers or they wouldn't have become sailors in the first place.

We have a complex system that feeds data into our brains to tell us who, what and where we are in this world. This system is part of our inheritance; genetics make it work.

One line of data is sent from the inner ear. There we have two mechanisms to tell our brain the position of our head. One is the semi-circular canal where fluids slosh around in response to motion. The other is the otoliths – stony, egg-shaped bits attached to hair cells and affected by gravity. More data comes from our eyes which constantly scan the horizon and our surroundings. And the third source is our proprioceptors, present in joints and muscles, which sense if anything is out of place on our body, sending signals that yes, your arm is in a certain position, even if you're not looking at it.

These information centres are constantly at work telling the brain everything's all right. The signals from one must confirm the three others; if one set of signals doesn't tally, we experience a conflict in our central nervous system. When our central nervous system goes out of whack, we turn pale, sweat, and feel nauseated. Those, in a nutshell, are the symptoms of seasickness.

Some people don't experience this while they're at sea – only after they get *off* the boat. Suddenly, the ground seems to be going up and down and the marina parking lot seems to be rolling in waves. Interestingly, these illusory waves roll at the same frequency as the real ones on the water.

Your body tells you the ground is undulating, and it isn't supposed to. Therefore this is much more unpleasant than watching real waves because real waves are meant to roll. Your brain is trying desperately to figure all this out and it isn't having too much luck. Your inner ear is trying to adjust to a rocking motion your eyes mistakenly perceive. There's definitely a loose cannon on your deck and it's making you feel none too well. You may not actually throw up, as you would on a real boat with real motion to contend with, but this trick your mind is playing on you is certainly no fun.

Genuine motion sickness (of which seasickness is just one variation) is a complex relationship between the various kinds of motion and the rate at which they change. On the water, there are angular, horizontal, and rotational accelerations. This is a lot of information for your brain to process. And, if you're unfortunate enough to be down below as all these changes are occurring, you are likely to be worse off than up on deck where you can at least fix on the horizon to steady your senses.

That's why pilots are better able to cope. They are heads-up people constantly looking at the horizon. The poor navigator with his head buried in the charts, or the bombardier in the cargo hold may have a simply terrible time. The worst place may be the engine room of a large ship where there are no external references at all.

If you are on board below decks, it's important to go up on deck from time to time to get your bearings. Looking through a porthole is not a good idea. You then have two conflicting visual references: the glass of the porthole may not be moving at the same rate or in the same direction as the water outside.

There are some very effective medications on the market, mostly of the antihistamine variety. They may make you a bit drowsy, but that's not a bad thing because, as some experienced sailors have learned, lying down and keeping your head still is a very good remedy. If you've ever seen someone lie down on a bunk and put pillows around his head to restrain motion, you've witnessed a very sophisticated method of dealing with the problem. It prevents the head's motions from being out of sync with those of the rest of the body and lessens the number of conflicting signals the brain receives.

There has been a lot of research into motion sickness, dating back to the beginning of World War II. Never before had so many people been moved across the seas. Troops who spent a week being transported by ship to their destination arrived in absolutely miserable condition. They had not been able to keep any food down for seven days, and they sometimes needed another whole week to recuperate. Those transported in cramped conditions on airplanes didn't fare much better.

Motion sickness became a very important topic for the military. As a result, a number of countries embarked upon very intensive research programmes. One of the most successful was carried out by Canada's Research Council. The Council constructed a variety of ingenious machines for testing theories. Some of these were so awful that in peacetime they might be considered instruments of torture!

These machines were capable of providing an incredible range of stimuli. They could tip, turn, and accelerate at the same time. The troops used as guinea pigs in the experiments must have comforted themselves with the thought that they were being sick for their country. They certainly provided invaluable assistance and their efforts were not in vain. The tests did indeed result in very effective remedies.

If you find the available remedies don't work well for you, there is still one way to overcome some of the ravages of seasickness. One of the worst aspects of not being able to keep food down is that you can become dehydrated and undernourished. If you'd rather be sailing even though it doesn't agree with you, keep nibbling on soft, mild foods at regular and frequent intervals. If you try to eat a lot at once, your stomach is going to bounce it all back. But this way you might be lucky enough to fool it into keeping some nourishment down.

The best remedy for seasickness I've personally encountered was one used by a friend. She had booked an extended sea voyage and discovered very quickly that this was a mistake. So she disembarked at the first port of call and flew back home.

THE JET SET

C offee, tea or milk? All three, advise some frequent fliers. Nothing, thanks, say others. Which is it to be? Some folks swear drinking lots of fluids will prevent jet lag. Others are equally convinced abstaining works.

They're all wrong. Fluids don't have anything to do with it. Jet lag can't be watered down. It is simply a matter of a biological clock ticking in each of our heads. We all run on a "diurnal cycle" which governs our patterns of sleep, wakefulness and the need for food. Our bodies may travel through time zones at the speed of sound, but our biological clocks stay set at the habits we have established at home. The three or five hours it takes to travel across a continent or an ocean isn't long enough for an adjustment.

If you were to travel between two cities in the same time zone four times in one day, you wouldn't feel jet-lagged. You might feel cooped up and somewhat confused, but your body would know when it was time to eat or go to bed. Jet lag, properly speaking, means your body is out of sync with where you are.

Drinking fluids isn't going to re-orient your body. And if you choose to drink fluids containing alcohol, you might jam up the works even more. Alcohol affects your sleep/waking cycles. When you drink it, it suppresses your wakefulness, and your brain becomes overactive to compensate. If you do manage to go to sleep, the hyperactivity will eventually wake you up – the reason your eyes sometimes open all by themselves at four in the morning after an evening of boozing. If you're already abusing your biological clock by changing time zones, adding a stiff drink is adding insult to injury.

Jet lag depends on which way you're going. If you're travelling north and south, you won't experience much trouble. But if you're flying from New York to Vancouver, you're going to be ready for supper when everyone else is sitting down to lunch. And it's not just because everyone on the West Coast is so laid back that they're always behind schedule!

You're going to be ready to hit the sack when they're just coming alive and when you wake up, the rest of Vancouver will still be asleep. Your body needs a few days to sort it all out. The trick is to start winding your clock back to Vancouver time before you get there.

Now, if you're a Vancouverite planning to travel east, you should start going to bed earlier and earlier every night, moving your clock forward. If you don't, you're going to lose most of a night's sleep once you arrive at your destination.

Most transatlantic flights from North America leave at night. You arrive in Europe at six a.m. local time when the world is just awakening. You temporarily forget that your body thinks it's one a.m., and you tend to try to spend the whole day taking in your new environment, perhaps visiting friends who, of course, are perfectly at ease with the time there and wouldn't think of going to bed at noon just to suit you. You forget that your sleep "bank" is being overdrawn and that you're incurring a large debt. Some time shortly after your arrival, your body is going to call in the loan. If you'd spent a few days moving your biological clock forward before you left, after a nap you'd be ready for local time when you woke up. But if you haven't previously made the adjustment, it's going to be very difficult.

Travelling from east to west always seems to take less toll on your system. You get the impression you've "gained" those three to five hours. The day is longer and you might not have too much trouble packing a bit more into it. Going the other way you "lose" the time and this can cause problems.

The next time I'm sent to England, I'll go gladly. As long as it's via Japan.

A RESTRAINING ORDER

I'd have been dead if I'd had my seat belt on!" There are some people who really believe that. They may have escaped a serious car accident without a scratch, and they make no bones about labelling seat belts dangerous.

Can *not* wearing your seat belt ever save your life? Once in a while the answer is "yes." The exception proves the rule. Sometimes someone is thrown clear of a car in an accident, escapes the injury of the collision, and is miraculously unscathed. Or sometimes, if he was wearing a seat belt, the only injuries received were from the seat belt.

But statistically these cases are very few and far between. If you are thrown clear of a vehicle at the time of impact, your chances of surviving without serious injury are slim. You're much safer in the car. Every once in a while someone does survive. It's a bit like playing Russian roulette. If I were playing Russian roulette with a six-shooter, I'd rather have five cylinders empty than five cylinders full. So I'd take my chances wearing a seat belt with the stats all on my side to begin with.

The people who say, "I escaped by not wearing my seat belt" are the few who are around to say it. Those who were thrown clear of their car and suffered either a crushed chest or, more likely, a crushed head, don't have a lot to tell us.

In the vast majority of accidents, seat belts prevent injury. When your car crashes into something, the impact causes you to crash into something else. Sometimes it's the steering wheel, sometimes it's the dashboard or another part of the car's interior. If you are thrown out of the car, you might hit the street curb or a lamp post or whatever is in the way. Wearing a seat belt confines the load of the impact to certain parts of your body. It distributes the force of the impact over a larger area than a specific target such as the windshield or the curb. It also prolongs the time of the impact because it stretches out as it restrains you. You might still hit the dashboard, but you'll hit it more slowly and with less force than if you were unrestrained.

It's true that a seat belt can hurt you. In an emergency room, doctors will often see seat belt injuries as part of the over-all trauma of a car crash. The injuries range from mild to serious bruises, from broken ribs to lacerations of the abdomen and bowel. In extreme and very rare circumstances, seat belts have been known to decapitate. If the collision was strong enough to cause these injuries, imagine what it would have done to the body if the person had not been wearing a seat belt.

Some drivers think that they need to wear their seat belts on the highway but can do without them in town. To a certain extent they are right. With a sudden stop at a speed of thirty kph, the kinetic energy in your body can be absorbed with less chance of harm. But at ninety kph, which is three times as fast, there is nine times as much kinetic energy to be absorbed. If it's absorbed by your steering wheel, it's going to be very painful.

One of my pet peeves is people who refuse to wear their seat belts in the back seat. For one thing, as the driver I am responsible for their safety but, more selfishly, in an accident, they could hurt *me* very badly. If they are thrown against the back of my seat, I am forced forward with the pressure on my chest increased as it hits the steering wheel or dashboard. Getting hurt as a passenger is bad enough, but killing the driver is downright inconsiderate.

It's too bad North American car manufacturers are reluctant to install shoulder belts (or for that matter, head rests) in back seats. Without a doubt, they offer much better protection than a lap belt alone. They would dramatically decrease incidents of whiplash because they can prevent a person's upper body and neck from snapping forward so suddenly.

I will allow that seat belts can pose problems for certain people, especially pregnant women who should buckle up not only for themselves but also for the child they are expecting. If a pregnant woman pitches forward, she may double up across her abdomen and risk the possibility of uterine rupture. The chances of the baby's surviving are very slim although the mother probably will.

Pregnant women quite rightly complain that seat belts are not designed to accommodate the mass they are carrying front and centre, and in the advanced stages of pregnancy, a seat belt can be uncomfortable if not impossible to put on. But it's still important to try – and important to get it on right. That means positioning the lap belt below the pelvic bones so that it won't cut into the abdomen in case of impact.

It's a pity so many people think seat belts are dispensable. Doctors all over North America have been one of the main lobbying groups urging mandatory seat belt use. They see it as an important health issue because they know from experience that seat belts can significantly reduce head and chest trauma. In places where seat belt legislation has been brought in, surveys have found that people still aren't convinced of the importance of buckling up. Eighty per cent of drivers strap themselves in after the laws are passed, but within months that figure goes down to fifty per cent. As a doctor, I just don't understand why half the population is willing to gamble with their lives.

CHAPTER TEN

Feeling
FIT

HURT ME, JANE FONDA!

Probably all those who are struggling to pound themselves into proper condition through exercise have heard the magic maxim: "No pain, no gain."

For all you locker-room masochists, I'm afraid the truth is that you *can* get fit without suffering very much. If you are suffering, you might be actually damaging yourself by over-exercising. Hurtin' ain't helpin'.

It's the old puritan ethic in action again: "I won't achieve anything if I don't suffer for it" or, "If I'm getting fit, it must mean the pain is good for me." Because most of us have done something that taxed us but which, in the end, made us more fit, we get used to the idea that suffering is a pre-condition to getting what we're after.

There are two kinds of pain we may experience when working out. One is soreness in the muscles the day after you've exerted yourself. Everybody knows what that's like. It's a fairly harmless discomfort usually gone within seventy-two hours and with little likelihood of causing permanent damage. Something as simple as a hot shower or bath may help ease the aches.

Pain that comes on suddenly as you're pumping that iron, however, may be due to a joint or a ligament strain, or, even more seriously, it could be related to cardiac problems. You have to respect sudden pain more than you do the morning-after muscle aches.

But let's not dismiss the morning-after muscle aches altogether. Suffering from them constantly could be a sign that you're taxing yourself, pushing yourself too hard. Good exercise programmes are graded to get you slowly into shape. You should work out only at the level you're capable of until your body's ready for the next round.

And don't forget that not all of you gets fit at the same rate. Your muscles may be bulging with new vitality fairly soon after you begin your exercise programme, but that doesn't mean your tendons, ligaments, and chest are ready yet for the Olympics. Your quadriceps can tolerate exercise long before the rest of you can, so you can't use them as a gauge on the road to fitness.

I hate to bring this up, but there's no question that age matters. A seventeen-year-old can abuse himself and get away with things that I, for one, just can't do anymore. It's sad to have to admit, but it's true. The young are more resilient. It takes less time for them to get into good condition, and they can do so with fewer risks of injury or disease.

Some pains are fairly common and nothing to get excited about. I don't think there is anyone who has never experienced a stitch, or a runner who has never had a shin splint.

A shin splint sounds terribly painful, and it does hurt. But it's not particularly damaging. It's just a sign of lack of oxygen in that part of the body. Runners know how to recognize it and they know that working through it isn't going to cause any harm.

Any other sharp, unexplained pain is a cue to cool it, especially if the pain occurs in your chest. Cardiac angina, or lack of oxygen to the heart, has been known to start up during a strenuous workout. Stop exercising and have a check-up before you start again.

Getting fit should also be a process of getting to know your body – and its limits. Extremely fit people, such as professional weight trainers, gymnasts, or ballet dancers, do suffer considerable discomfort from time to time. They learn to balance the discomfort against the level of excellence they wish to achieve. They also learn the difference between fatigue and pain. They know that aching muscles and tendons are uncomfortable but tolerable, and they develop a sixth sense that tells them when they've pushed too far.

So unless you're working towards a gold medal in masochism, quit when it hurts.

A MESSAGE FROM MOTHER NATURE

Picture this scenario: you have got a regular exercise programme you never miss. Say you jog a mile or swim twenty laps. Then one day you feel a touch of the flu or you twist your ankle a bit. What to do?

You continue to run or swim. You just keep going. Right?

A definite "no" to running during an illness; a qualified "no" to running with an injury. You should definitely not work out when you are sick. And if you have an injury, you should seek professional advice before you continue your exercise programme.

Let's look at the illness first. The most common illnesses we get are flu and colds. They may be trivial enough not to keep you from your normal daily activities, but they do put your body under stress. The viruses that cause them affect not only your head but your entire body. Every cell is afflicted. With this considerable stress on your system, it doesn't make any sense for you to add more stress by pushing your body to the limit. You can't expect your body to perform feats of physical prowess when it would rather be prone, drinking chicken soup, and watching the soaps. So don't beat yourself up if you discover all that training hasn't made you superhuman. Exercise may keep you generally healthier, but it's not a vaccination against viruses.

Moderate exercise may be beneficial for a minor ailment such as a cold. You don't have to hibernate, but if you're accustomed to running a mile a day, when you have a cold you might find that you're tired at half a mile. That's Mother Nature's way of telling you that's enough for one day. Listen to her.

When it comes to injuries, Mother Nature's messages often come through loud and clear. If you've twisted your ankle while running, the message usually says, "Boy, that hurts!" If the pain doesn't go away quickly, it's time to seek some advice. Many trainers and physiotherapists are experts with these injuries. Let them set your pace back onto the track.

There are some injuries you can't afford to ignore unless you want to risk turning them into a chronic condition. If you've injured a ligament or a tendon and you continue to stress it, it may not heal properly. You're going to live with that tendon or ligament for the rest of your life: give it a chance to spring back and be of good service to you in the long run.

Runners commonly develop all sorts of conditions in their ligaments and tendons, around their bones, and in their muscles. Heel spurs, for example, are very common. So is tendonitis. If you have one of these running-associated problems and you continue to flog it, it's going to get worse and it could keep you from running – permanently. Preventing the problem or getting it treated before you continue with your exercise is only sensible.

Good old common sense can't compete with our sports mythology. There's the baseball catcher who succeeds at a phenomenal play on a broken ankle and is (rightly) lionized after the game. There's the NFL lineman who breaks his clavicle but continues to barge on to take out the opposing quarterback. These are astonishing feats of human endurance. They should be applauded for the rare and amazing achievements they are, but I really don't recommend such heroics as a lifestyle.

If you want to know where this mythology leads, try to see a great old movie called *North Dallas Forty.* In it, Nick Nolte plays an aging professional football player whose body is nothing more than a collection of scars, wounds, and old injuries that have never healed. In order to keep the pain level down, he has to have his Vitamin B12 shot before every game.

The whole point of exercise, as I see it, is to get fit and to stay fit. Wrecking bits and pieces of yourself as you go strikes me as the opposite of that idea.

ON THE ROAD TO RECOVERY

If you have the misfortune to have a heart attack, the odds for your survival are fairly good. But conventional wisdom has it that you never fully recover, that the quality of your lifestyle will inevitably decrease.

It's just not true. You *can* lead a normal life after a heart attack. You can also lead a fit life after a heart attack, especially if you follow an appropriate rehabilitation programme.

It's true your heart will never be the same. The essence of a heart attack is that a portion of the heart muscle dies. It can be a very tiny portion of the heart or a fairly large one. The heart responds by filling in the area with scar tissue.

You still have a lot of reserve function left in the old ticker. It's a little weaker, sometimes imperceptibly, and there is some permanent damage but that doesn't mean you can't lead a full life.

Age, as it so often does, makes a difference. It's true that the younger you are, the better you get over an injury. There is an interesting effect of age, however, that most people aren't aware of.

The heart muscle is supplied by various large arteries. They are interlinked by a network of tiny vessels called "collateral arteries." We are all born with a certain number of collaterals, the number varying from individual to individual. With age, the collaterals tend to enlarge. An older person having a heart attack might have better collateral circulation than a younger one. When the artery shuts off at the top, the collaterals pick up the slack at the bottom, providing a better blood flow and, therefore, less damage. A sixty-two-year-old suffering a heart attack may actually suffer less damage than a forty-two-year-old.

The amount of damage caused by a heart attack is the main factor in recovery. There are, sadly, cases where the damage is too extensive. But the second most important factor is attitude. You can be a "cardiac cripple" when, although the physical prognosis is good, you're convinced that life isn't worth living. If you feel a shadow hanging over you and worry that everything you do will lead to disaster, it could become a self-fulfilling prophecy. That's why rehab programmes which teach you that you Can Do are often very helpful and important.

There are also some very real physical steps you need to take to ensure your continuing progress. The first is to stop smoking. If you don't stop, you are surely going to have another attack.

The next is to reduce your blood pressure. You may not have known before the attack that your blood pressure was too high, but now you do and you have to get it down. Drug therapies for this are important. Appropriate exercise will also help.

Every once in a while, a tragic statistic comes along that makes us wonder what really does work. A few years ago, Jim Fixx, one of the biggest proponents of running as a way of preventing heart disease, died of a heart attack while jogging. The scepticism that resulted from this high-profile death was, in my opinion, quite unjustified – as unjustified as were all the oversold benefits of running before he died.

It's important to remember that there was a long history of heart attacks in Fixx's family. His father had died of a heart attack at a fairly early age. If your great-grandfather succumbed before age forty, and your grandfather, father, and one of your brothers are already dead, you have good reason to fear for your own mortality. You can't outrun genetics.

But in general, fitness does help people recover. If you were fit before you suffered the attack, you'll heal faster after it. There is no guarantee against heart attacks, but there is reason to believe that being fit decreases their incidence.

The problem arises when people blame themselves for the crisis. After an attack, they look inward and question their values, their fundamental attitudes and attributes. If you are a smoker, then you are in fact somewhat to blame for the situation. However, even if you have been an abstainer all your life, have followed a healthy diet, and know you have good genes, you could still experience an attack. Nothing reduces your risk to zero.

We have to live with the cards we were dealt. But if we make the most of them by not smoking, eating right and staying in good condition, we might find we hold a winning hand.

A LONG HARD NIGHT

Have you got a back ache? Maybe your bed's too soft. Everyone knows that hard beds are better for your back. But are they really? Only if you love to suffer. Otherwise, I don't think so.

The softest bed you can have is a hammock; the hardest, a slab of concrete. Somewhere in between, there's a bed that's just right for you.

A hammock supports you at your head and your heels. In between, you're twisted up like a pretzel. That's not good for your joints, especially the tiny little back joints about five millimetres wide that spend all night being scrunched. If you're all twisted up, the muscles, ligaments and tendons that hold your bones together are over-stretched on one side and over-compressed on the other. It's not surprising then that, when you get up, your body, and especially your back, is out of kilter.

A solid, hard-as-a-rock bed, on the other hand, supports you only where you stick out, that is, at your head, shoulders, and pelvis. The in-between parts get no support at all. You might say they never rest. You could spend all night rolling over, trying to give those parts a bit of comfort, and wake up exhausted from your efforts.

Doctors can take the blame for this particular myth. Not too long ago, when most people's beds were of poor quality, doctors would see many patients complaining about bad backs. A few examples were all it took for doctors to conclude that sway-back beds were causing the problem. After all, a lumpy mattress won't provide much more support than a hammock. The solution became clear: a firmer bed.

The easiest way to achieve this was to put a flat board under the mattress. The improvement was dramatic.

Nowadays, when almost everyone owns a modern box spring, there's very little excuse for having a sway-back bed. A good bed provides not only a solid underpinning but also some surface softness that allows the bony prominences of skinny people like me to sink in comfortably.

Many people swear by waterbeds for the most comfortable sleep since the princess found her pea. Waterbeds don't get softer with time unless you let the water out. And it's difficult to inflate a waterbed improperly: if you're bottoming out when you climb on, you'll know that you haven't put enough water in. Filled up correctly, a waterbed can provide general support without too much surface hardness.

Doctors routinely ask back patients what sort of bed they're sleeping on. Most say, "My bed is fine, thank you." But every once in a while when we encounter a recalcitrant back, it pays to go have a look at the patient's bed – for purely professional reasons, of course.

Although doctors don't often make house calls in bad back cases, people with back pain have been known to become so crippled they can't go out. So we have to go and have a look. And, sure enough, they've been sleeping on the same bed for twenty to twenty-five years and they've been "comfortable," so why shouldn't they be comfortable now? One look at the bed and the answer is obvious.

Be like Goldilocks and don't settle for a bed that's too hard or too soft. Your body will tell you when it's just right.

THE COLD WATER PLUNGE

Leaping into cold water after a hot sauna is bracing. Some people say it's invigorating, other people think it's nuts. These latter point to a popular notion that taking the plunge can cause heart failure. But let's not leap to conclusions.

People have been cooling off for probably thousands of years, if not more, and most have survived just fine. But once in a very rare while there is not a happy ending and the consequences might be fatal.

Your heart basically operates as an electrical mechanism. You have a natural pacemaker firing off electrical charges into the heart at regular intervals, making the muscle contract. The system operates automatically rather well without any other control. However, it is subject to override from your central nervous system.

In a hot sauna, your nerves are thoroughly stimulated in one direction. Then, you jump into cold water and give them a jolt in the opposite direction. This could, in an extreme case, cause a circuit overload and stop your pacemaker from firing off again. Your heart might be in great condition, but the problem isn't a mechanical one: it's electrical. Your age or degree of fitness doesn't make much difference.

I've encountered only one case like this, and that's probably a lifetime quota. A young man who had just finished his fellowship exams in orthopaedic surgery went on holiday with a group of friends who had also passed their exams. They all went into the hotel sauna and then he jumped into the pool. He suffered cardiac arrest, and, despite the fact that all his friends present were doctors, no one could resuscitate him.

Even without a sauna first, there is always a risk attendant on jumping into cold water. Heart attacks have been known to happen to people forced to jump off a sinking ship or to exit from an airplane that has crashed into the sea. If the water is cold enough the temperature difference can kill.

I have to admit that with advancing age I am becoming more of "a chicken." I never jump headlong into a pool any more if I can avoid it. Leaping in on a hot summer day probably won't cause any harm but when I come out of a sauna, I walk into the pool slowly. You don't need a ten-minute ease-in; sixty seconds is enough. But a gradual immersion seems to protect you.

Now isn't that what our parents advised us to do when we were kids? Isn't it amazing how wise they seem now that we're all a bit older?

CHAPTER ELEVEN

The Sexy
BITS

Part I: Men

SCORING BEFORE THE BIG GAME

O kay, sports fans. I'm willing to tackle just about any myth. There's one that sex before the big game hurts performance – on the field, that is.

I suppose it will if you believe it will. And if you don't believe it, it won't. There have always been athletes who swore off sex as part of their training. I'm sure you've heard of the great boxer who doesn't indulge for a couple of weeks before the title round so that he won't sap his "vital energies." On the other hand, athletes like Joe Namath put the notion to the test and found it fallacious.

So how was the connection made between dissipating one's energies in bed and being dissipated on the field the next day? I have some theories on the subject and I'm willing to go toe-to-toe with anyone who disagrees with them.

Part of being a good athlete is having a good coach. The coach, rightly, sees winning as depending not only on the athlete's ability to chuck a spear or jump a distance but also on his mental and physical well-being. A good coach manages every aspect of his charge's life in order to prepare him for peak athletic performance. This management can be very personal, including what the athlete eats, how much he sleeps, what he drinks and, not surprisingly, when he has sex. Personal management can get very personal indeed.

Sexual abstinence is a form of discipline and, of course, the athlete has to be a very disciplined individual. There is no better discipline than that of an athlete in a training programme.

Sex doesn't take a lot of energy, certainly not for someone in peak physical condition. A professional hockey player or Olympic runner should be able to tolerate it better than most of us. And after sex, there is a languid feeling most of us appreciate.

Could that nice feeling of being at peace with the world interfere with the aggressiveness that some sports such as football and boxing demand? I think not. A football player or a boxer has to know how to exhibit aggression at the appropriate times, to channel it into his sport. Any athlete who can't confine his battling instincts to the field or ring is a danger.

There is a mental connection most of us make between the male hormone, testosterone, and aggressive behaviour. It might seem logical to assume that sex changes the testosterone level and reduces aggressiveness. But this would be a wrong assumption. Sex doesn't affect the hormone level appreciably. And besides, someone who is naturally aggressive is likely to be sexually aggressive as well. You can't argue that he is draining away his precious testosterone when what he is doing is exhibiting aggressive behaviour. It just doesn't wash.

It's interesting that it's only male athletes who seem to worry about sapping their vital energies. You certainly never hear anyone advocating that female athletes abstain. So it may all just be part of a big mystique. If you've ever been around a boxer preparing for a fight, you'd get the impression he was about to be ordained as a monk. Because so much of boxing is *attitude*, perhaps all this rigmarole is just tonic for the psyche.

I'm going to go out on a limb and suggest that sex before a big game might even be beneficial. It certainly results in a good frame of mind and that can't hurt. Besides, as an exercise it sure beats skipping rope.

IT'S HIS TIME OF LIFE

Is there such a thing as a male menopause? There are an equal number of people who believe there is and believe there isn't. I believe there is.

The problem is that it is not an exact parallel to a woman's menopause. A woman going through her change of life might, rightly, look at a middle-aged man and complain, "You ain't got nothing on me, Charlie!" And it's true because there is nothing obviously dramatic going on in his body. He doesn't have disturbances in his hormone cycle, a severe drop in hormone levels, irregular menses, or hot flashes. Women experience all these things – and they know, because they suffer as a result, that it's a serious and often uncomfortable series of events. How dare some man pretend he too is suffering?

Perhaps the trouble lies in calling the changes a man goes through in middle life by the same name. "Mena," after all, is a properly female prefix that appears in *men*arche and *men*struation. I concur with those who call a man's situation "metapause." *Meta* means change, as in *meta*morphosis.

Men experience metapause around the same age as women experience menopause, perhaps starting a bit earlier and lasting a bit longer. On the average, women go through their change of life between forty-five and fifty. You rarely see a menopausal woman as young as thirty-five, nor one as old as fifty-seven. Men can start to change at forty and keep changing until sixty or beyond.

Men do not have hormone cycles to begin with, so there's nothing to become irregular and finally stop. But they do experience a gradual reduction in hormone levels which does have some physical manifestations. Perhaps, more importantly, a man's metapause causes psychological changes.

When a man reaches forty-five, he finds himself in one of two situations. Either he has become very successful and realizes he has reached his goals or he is not successful and realizes he has gone as far as he's going to go. Both situations can create a sense of aimlessness, a crisis of Where Do I Go From Here?

Now enter the blonde and the convertible. His marriage may be less satisfying, both emotionally and physically, than it was fifteen years ago. And he says, "Hey! Nothing that a sexy young woman and a young man's car can't fix!" When I turned forty, I bought myself a bright red Thunderbird. It was my way of breaking out of the rut. I did, however, stay married to the same woman.

Did it change my life? Not a bit.

A lot of things that happen at this age – for both men and women – are heavily psychological. There are changes in expectations, of course, but also changes caused by declining abilities including sexual ones. There are changing relationships with children including the "empty nest syndrome" which shifts the emphasis back to the couple for the first time in twenty years.

Women are, in a sense, fortunate because their physical changes can be helped medically with hormone treatments. This therapy is relatively easy and it works. But there are a lot of other things that a pill won't remedy. For men, we don't have any pills at all but we should pay the same kind of attention to what's going on in their heads.

There is one kind of "medicine" available, but its success depends on the man's willingness and ability to take it. It involves being aware of what's going on and not waiting for things to start tumbling down around his head. Too many men are "proud," in the sense that they don't want to admit something is wrong and seek outside counselling and independent advice. They just blunder through – sometimes making mistakes in judgement that hurt themselves and their loved ones.

My prescription for metapause is to be aware of it and prepare to make an assessment of your life. It's not a myth. It needs to be met head on.

Part II: Women

HER TIME OF MONTH

Your period's coming. You're feeling positively icky. Your breasts are tender and you feel bloated. You feel anxious and depressed. Is it like this for all women? Or are you a victim of Pre-Menstrual Syndrome?

There are pre-menstrual symptoms which are very real. And there is Pre-Menstrual Syndrome which is also very real. PMS is defined as significant symptoms that occur regularly in the same phase of the menstrual cycle, end with the onset of menses and disappear completely for at least one week after menses. But the question is: what is a "significant" symptom?

One of the symptoms of PMS is breast swelling. But forty per cent of all women have swollen breasts before their periods. Another symptom is weight gain or water retention. Eighty per cent of women experience that. A majority of women also experience one or several of the following: irritability, depression, lack of energy, reduction in sexual interest, headaches, urinary frequency, changes in appetite, a craving for carbohydrates, insomnia, and so on.

There isn't any magic number or combination of symptoms that adds up to PMS. If you ask women if they have any of these symptoms and they say "Yes," and then ask them if they have PMS, many will say "No." Some women who have identified themselves as PMS sufferers may have fewer distinct symptoms. It's really a question of personal tolerance. PMS can be identified objectively, but ultimately it's a matter of whether the woman can live with her discomforts. If she can't, no matter how few or how many symptoms she has, she can fairly be said to suffer from PMS.

PMS was first identified in the 1930s. We have known about it and treated it as a serious condition for the last fifty years. But recently it has become trendy. I am not too sure why PMS in particular has become fashionable, but I do think there has been a tendency in the last decade to identify clusters of symptoms and put them under an umbrella labelled "syndrome." This brings out the True Believers who latch onto it as an explanation for everything.

But let's look at one particular symptom of PMS more closely. There are different degrees of chronic anxiety, depression, and psychological disturbance. It's easy to blame PMS. In some cases these may not be due to PMS at all but to ongoing stress. Even though anxiety may peak in the pre-menstrual period, it should be treated for the whole month, not just for the two weeks when it's at its most intolerable.

PMS has been used as a rationale for everything. In England, it has even been used successfully as a defence in criminal trials of aggravated assault. The principal witness in these trials was a doctor who is the prime champion of PMS and who believes it is caused by a deficiency of progesterone. She has promoted progesterone supplements very heavily, creating a climate that, in my opinion, amounts to indiscriminate drug use.

I could quote a dozen equally erudite theories about what causes PMS and how it should be treated, all of them propounded by excellent people. What that tells me is that nobody really knows. The progesterone theory has some merit because we do know that progesterone and estrogen levels decrease prior to menses. But genetic factors are equally convincing because there does seem to be a family tendency in some women. We also mustn't ignore social stress caused by sexual stereotypes.

PMS might be alleviated after a pregnancy. Or it might increase. Oral contraceptives, too, may make PMS better or worse. There are no easy answers. Any treatments we have right now are temporary and need to be used repeatedly. For moderate symptoms, self-help is the most hopeful route right now. You should steer clear of medical therapies for as long as you can. It's valuable to confer with a medical person for reassurance that your symptoms are normal and not an indication of some impending disaster. Then, learn to identify when and how you are affected and calculate a strategy for dealing with it.

Some doctors help this process by asking you to record your ups and downs over a few months. This chart is useful in helping to determine whether you do indeed suffer from PMS and also makes you feel involved in your own treatment. It has as much psychotherapeutic value as physical value.

Part of your self-help, then, is to seek reassurance. Another part is diet. You can lower your cravings for carbohydrates by eating small, frequent meals of high nutritional value such as pastas and bread instead of sugar. Some people swear by vitamins, especially B6. Although there is absolutely no clinical evidence that B6 has any effect, at least it's harmless.

Evening primrose oil is another substance being peddled as a nostrum. It has become such big business in North America that farmers have turned over entire fields to growing primroses. I don't buy it.

What I do buy is exercise and stress management. Counselling to help you and your family through rough times is valuable. So is relaxation therapy.

If you suffer bloating to the point that your ankles swell like tree trunks and you can't get your jeans over your tummy, diuretics or water pills can help. Your doctor should prescribe them for short-term use. A trial of oral contraceptives is a good idea, too. You'll know within a few cycles if it works. If it doesn't, it doesn't. But if it does, it's wonderful.

If you're really troubled, try the progesterone therapy. Remember, it has to be injected or taken as a vaginal suppository, so you can't do it without a doctor. I personally don't prescribe it, but it has been known to benefit some people.

A DILL PICKLE SUNDAE, TO GO

So the little woman suddenly starts craving dill pickles and ice cream? Well, fellah, you'd better start stocking up on diapers. That sort of strange appetite can mean only one thing: she's pregnant.

This is one of my favourite myths, celebrated in song and story and tacky television sitcoms, that pregnant women have strange food cravings deep into the night. And you know something? It's true.

The phenomenon is known as "pica," or an abnormal appetite. It applies to anyone with strange food cravings, not just pregnant women. It is not nearly as common as we all believe, but when it happens and it happens to you, it is very real.

We don't know why pica occurs, but I'm willing to speculate. We all know that pregnancy alters the hormonal mix in your body. We don't totally understand our chemistry, but we do know that hormones affect the appetite. The body tends to crave what it thinks it needs to nourish itself.

Research has shown, for example, that if you allow children to eat whatever they want and make a wide selection of food available to them, they will amaze you by picking out a fairly balanced diet. The body knows what it wants — most of the time.

There have been case histories of children who are calcium deficient found nibbling dry wall or chalk. There are examples of people who lose salt because their kidneys are diseased who develop cravings for all manner of salty things. Women having their periods have been known to eat laundry starch or shovel sugar down by the spoonful. These may seem like irrational cravings, but I suspect the body has its own reasons for the occasional odd appetite.

I know of one woman who had a real appetite for paperback books. She just ate them up – literally. It struck everyone as bizarre until doctors discovered she had a certain mineral deficiency which was being satisfied by the paperback consumption. When the problem was corrected by her physician, her behaviour pattern returned to normal.

Women who develop weird tastes during pregnancies may have had perfectly normal appetites before. A perfectly sane, rational person may start downing the most incredible things because her hormonal stew needs some mysterious seasoning.

Pica, when it appears in a pregnancy, will usually surface during the first trimester. There's always one woman who knows she is pregnant even though she hasn't yet missed a period because she's hungry for things she hasn't wanted since her last pregnancy. For most women, though, pica appears towards the end of the first trimester and usually disappears by the end of the second.

Much more common during pregnancy than cravings is the opposite, a revulsion towards certain kinds of food. Fat sensitivity is one example. Some pregnant women get sick at the mere thought of fatty foods. Some women go off *all* food because there is reason to believe that the hormone levels associated with pregnancy slow the digestion process and make them feel full almost all the time.

There are two beneficial revulsions that sometimes occur during a pregnancy. One is a distaste for alcohol. A normal drinker who likes the occasional glass of wine may suddenly find membership in the Temperance Union very appealing. I encourage this attitude in my patients because fetal alcohol syndrome can be very serious and occurs at far lower levels than we ever thought possible.

The other revulsion is towards cigarettes. A pregnant woman who smokes may suddenly find she's nauseated by the smell of cigarette smoke. I'm glad when this happens because, as we all know, not smoking is good and doubly so during a pregnancy.

So bear with the lady whose tastes strike you as peculiar. Fetch her the baked eggplant stuffed with peanut butter at one in the morning. Bring her some goat's milk to wash it down with. And smile when you're at a restaurant and she orders horseradish on crackers while turning down the Pouilly Fuissé.

AT A MOTHER'S BREAST

Here's a notion that's come full circle. It used to be that large numbers of people believed that breastfeeding acted as a natural contraceptive. The idea has been widely discredited and now, very few still believe it. But the pendulum has swung too far in the opposite direction. Breastfeeding *can* prevent another pregnancy. It's certainly not adequate contraception, but it does work occasionally.

Fertility is a function of hormone cycles. Think of your hormones as waves on a lake, going up and down. When the waves are high, you are capable of ovulation. When the waves are low, you menstruate. The whole system is controlled by a command centre known as the pituitary gland.

When a woman is suckling an infant, a reflex in her breast sends a message to the pituitary which interrupts the hormone cycle. It builds a dam on the lake. If the hormone levels don't rise and fall, ovulation won't occur. And if she doesn't ovulate, she can't get pregnant.

The problem, of course, is that if a woman doesn't ovulate for a while, she is lulled into thinking she is "safe." She may have experienced the contraceptive effect of breastfeeding for months, even a year, and then suddenly she's pregnant. She had no way of knowing that her hormones had broken through the dam.

Obviously, this is not a reliable method of contraception and probably the reason it has been so widely discredited. For some women it doesn't work at all. For others, it works part of the time – but they don't know when.

It works least well for North American women. It works best for women in societies we consider "primitive." In those societies, the idea of separating a mother and infant is unthinkable. But we demand interruptions in the breastfeeding cycle. We have work and social commitments which lead us to say, "Let's add an occasional bottle," or "Let's change feeding times." These variations give the hormones a chance to kick in. Breastfeeding interruptus is about as reliable a contraceptive as coitus interruptus.

Mother Nature thought up this grand scheme to ensure survival of the species. In many parts of the world, a mother's milk may be an infant's only source of protein, calories, and certain vitamins that she can digest and absorb. In poor countries, the child's survival may depend on her mother's ability to breastfeed her until she is two-and- a-half or three.

When I was practising in West Africa, I saw children die because their mothers became pregnant again. Pregnancy causes the milk supply to dry up. A six, nine or thirteen months old infant isn't ready to be weaned, but suddenly there is no more food available. And even if the infant survives the transition from mother's milk to gruel or porridge, he may die of malnutrition a few years down the line.

This is why I think breastfeeding is designed to prevent another pregnancy – to protect the child already born. But obviously, it doesn't work perfectly. The most heartbreaking case I saw was a couple who came to the clinic begging us to prevent any further pregnancies. They had had twenty-three children of whom only two had survived. They knew what the problem was: they had seen the woman's milk dry up when she got pregnant. So they desperately wanted to give the most recent child a chance.

We did a tubal ligation, and afterwards the man fell to the ground and kissed my feet. I was somewhat taken aback, but I realized this was the local expression of profound gratitude.

Mother Nature doesn't always get it right. But her instincts are good.

Part III: Babies

MIS-CONCEPTION

There are lots of myths about getting pregnant. But the biggest one is this: it's easy.

A boy and girl of eighteen have sex for the very first time and wham! – she's pregnant. Literature and films would have us believe it's even easier than *that*. In *Tess of the D'Urbervilles,* the heroine falls asleep under a tree and wakes up "with child," as they used to say. In *Agnes of God,* the young novice's pregnancy is the result of a dove descending on her. Wonder of wonders!

In real life, however, most of us who have children know that conception is far more difficult. And if the first child came easily, the second one may be harder to conceive. If this weren't true, we wouldn't be seeing thousands of infertility clinics all over the world.

Age is a big factor. Today, for a variety of personal reasons, a lot of couples wait to have a child. There is no doubt fertility does decline with age. A woman in her thirties may have a difficult time getting pregnant. A woman of forty may find it impossible. Men are potent a bit longer, but there is no doubt that younger is better for the task at hand.

The reproductive system is so complex that there is always a possibility of glitches. And as the system ages, the variety and subtlety of glitches grow exponentially.

The more time goes by, of course, the more chances there are of a woman contracting some of the serious pelvic infections that can lead to sterility. These include chlamydia and old-fashioned gonorrhea. A woman's contraceptive history may also play a role. A thirty-six-year-old woman who has been using a contraceptive device for eighteen of her reproductive years may have damaged her system. The most obvious case is that of an IUD, which is known to pose serious risk of ascending infection.

The Pill is quite safe from this problem, but it takes some time after going off it to re-establish a normal hormonal cycle. And the longer you've been taking the Pill, the longer it may take your body to revert to normal.

When a doctor sees a couple not achieving the desired results, he finds that the most common mistake they make is trying too hard. They have increased the frequency of intercourse – thinking the more shots at it, the better. But frequent intercourse could result in a lower sperm count.

Chances are that the couple is putting too much pressure on conception. It's true that being uptight works against you. There's that old chestnut about a wise, old country doctor who advises a young couple who have been trying unsuccessfully, to adopt a child. They do and, three months later, bingo! – she's pregnant. It sounds unlikely, but in fact it happens too often to dismiss as a myth. There may be something about mothering and nurturing a child that decreases any uptightness which has prevented conception. I don't pretend to understand it, but I do believe it.

In a hundred infertile couples, the chances of the problem being something wrong with the man would be one-third. The chances of there being something wrong with the woman would be two-thirds. Occasionally, there may be nothing wrong with either one, but they don't succeed. Her chemistry isn't compatible with his, but that's exceedingly rare.

Fortunately, for most people it's simply a matter of timing. The day or two before ovulation is the time to concentrate on getting pregnant. During the week after your period, there's no egg around to fertilize. The week before your period, the egg has been and gone.

The trick is to focus activity on that one week a month when conception is possible, but it's not a time to go bananas. Limit your love making to every other day. Expecting a man's body to churn out the sperm day after day after day after day may put too high a demand on the quality of his production.

If there is still a problem, first get the male checked out. His equipment is relatively simple and taking a sperm count is easy. A woman's system is far more complex and requires so much more probing and poking that she's bound to be uncomfortable. It's a lot simpler for all concerned to get the man in or out of contention as the source of the problem. When a couple come to see me, the very first thing I ask for is a semen analysis. If there are lots of sperm and they're alive and wiggling, then, and only then, do you know you have to look elsewhere.

Few people who find themselves in this situation are naive about how and when it all works. Sex education has been beneficial in that respect. Also, when a couple makes up their minds to Do It, chances are they'll become interested in the subject and read up on it. That doesn't mean they don't still indulge in some weird practices.

There are still some old wives' tales around that certain sexual positions will guarantee a boy and some new wives' tales, with a very scientific veneer, that sperm which swim sideways will produce girls or some such rubbish. I had a colleague who swore he could predict a baby's sex; I challenged him with a bet on the next baby he delivered. I had a fifty per cent chance of winning – and I did win. Mind you, I also had a fifty per cent chance of losing.

We do know that you can centrifuge semen to produce a concentration of sperm which contain either the X or Y chromosome. Veterinarians do this with success in breeding cattle. But cows aren't people, and I don't want to create the notion that it's a simple procedure that can be easily adapted to human beings. Choosing the sex of your child still belongs in the realm of science fiction and I, for one, would like to keep it there.

THE STORK DELIVERS AT MIDNIGHT

If you are expecting a child there is at least one other thing you can expect: a late night trip to the hospital because, as everybody knows, babies are usually born in the small hours.

The literature clearly states that there is a uniform distribution of birth times throughout the day but I have a hard time believing it. I've delivered babies for years and, in my experience, the little wretches seem almost always to show up when it's pitch black outside.

I will admit this may be a misconception, if you will pardon my pun. An average labour lasts twelve to fourteen hours, and chances are either the beginning or the end will occur at night time, because the day is, after all, only twenty-four hours long. In addition, everyone remembers the baby born at four a.m. If I go down to the hospital at two in the afternoon, well, ho-hum, it's two in the afternoon. But if the phone rings at my bedside at four in the morning, I'm going to remember the little devil who interrupted my sleep just because he was ready to join the world. And looking back over a period of three months, I'll remember each time I was awakened in the middle of the night whereas the afternoon births will fade from memory.

The more I read about it, the less certain I am that I understand the mechanism that triggers a woman's labour. I think it is a complex combination of factors that medical science hasn't altogether figured out. But I know the sun setting isn't one of them.

Understanding labour is extremely important. It's an area of very active research. We know that premature labours can be a disaster; they are still the cause of a lot of mortality and morbidity. Late labours can be equally distressing, but they are more easily managed because you have an option of getting the baby out by Caesarean section. Knowing how labour works is a key to having healthy babies.

It is true that first babies are more often overdue than subsequent babies. It's almost as though the body gets the hang of it after a while. There aren't too many women these days having six or seven babies, but those who do definitely deliver the sixth or seventh a lot faster and more easily than the first. I once delivered a thirteenth baby. It slipped out like a seal.

But in all fairness, "due dates" can be misleading. They are meant as an ETA, not an exact time of arrival. A due date is usually accurate within a plus or minus of two weeks. A baby born two weeks before a due date is not considered premature, nor is one born two weeks after a due date really late.

Normal, healthy babies carried by a normal, healthy woman come out when they're ready. There is a notion, mostly in books and films, that a shock or trauma can trigger a labour. It is possible, but the only place I've ever encountered it was in *Wuthering Heights*. In real life, I have known women who experienced a shock, such as a car accident, but didn't deliver until their time.

False labour, on the other hand, is common and an embarrassment for everybody. The woman rings all the alarms, everyone gathers round, the whole world goes into an uproar ... and nothing happens. After a couple of times, she's afraid to cry "Wolf!" again.

In all fairness, doctors aren't very helpful in these situations. The attending physician might get a bit testy the fourth time around. But the truth of the matter is that the only difference between real labour and false labour is that one results in a delivery and the other doesn't.

At the onset, there is almost no way to tell. If the labour doesn't progress, it's easy to say, in retrospect, that it was a false labour. But it seemed like the real thing at the time and a doctor should treat it as though it were.

There is one consolation: false labours don't go on forever. Eventually one of the labours is going to pay off. Probably at four a.m.

The Whole
PERSON

SWEATING IT OUT

I f you give me fever (through the morning and all through the night), the least you could do is pile some blankets on me and help me sweat it out. Those aren't the *exact* lyrics of Peggy Lee's famous song, but a lot of people sing these words.

This is a dangerous myth. There once was a school of medical thought that believed in inducing fever to help cure certain diseases. Most of the physicians who prescribed it are now dead, although it's not certain that they died of their own therapy. Fortunately, the concept of fighting fire with fire has been totally discredited.

A fever is your body's ordinary, and usually effective, response to an infection. Because an infection, interestingly enough, makes your body feel cold, it raises its internal thermostat to compensate. The effect is exactly the same as running stark naked into a snow storm: your peripheral circulation contracts to prevent heat loss, your metabolism speeds up, and you shiver. Shivering is purposeless muscle contraction – an attempt to generate heat.

When the body gets the temperature up, it registers on the thermometer as a fever. Now your body says, "I feel too hot." It lowers the thermostat and goes through a series of steps to get the temperature back to normal. You turn beet red as your peripheral circulation dilates, you sweat, and your heart races to pump the circulation through the skin faster.

If we pile the blankets on, we keep the heat in and force it even higher. An adult, at worst, will feel uncomfortable. But for a child, doing this could be downright dangerous. Children have a higher ratio of brain mass to body weight: when their metabolism speeds up and their brain's needs can't be met they frequently go into convulsions – a very serious medical emergency.

On the face of it, it seems to make sense to keep the temperature climbing until it gets to the top and starts to fall. But piling on the blankets is folly because your chances of overshooting the mythical "top" are one hundred per cent. All you do is turn yourself into a very efficient heat generator, with very little heat loss.

Fevers usually have a pattern that lasts from four to six hours. You'll get through one fever only to discover that six hours later the mercury is climbing again. But it's not a catastrophe. If you know to expect a cycle, you can plan to make the next rise more tolerable.

For adults, a fever at the onset of a cold or flu will last one or two days. The best remedy is those old standbys, Aspirin and acetaminophen. But you have to know their limits. They will lower the temperature only by one to one-and-a-half degrees celsius – not all the way down to normal. You won't be "cured," but you will probably feel more comfortable.

For children the remedy is the same, but I would recommend steering clear of Aspirin because of its potential implication in Reye's syndrome. Also, don't be afraid to cool the child down.

Anxious parents bring a convulsing child down to the hospital emergency room bundled up in sweaters and hooded jackets. They are horrified when the doctors and nurses rip everything off and either put a great big fan across the child's bare skin or plunge her into ice-cold water.

It seems brutal, but if the child is convulsing she is unconscious and needs drastic treatment. There is always the danger of permanent neurological damage. Fortunately, the vast majority of convulsions, if handled properly, don't have any long-term effects.

If your child has a fever at home and has not begun to convulse, don't be afraid to set a fan up next to the bed. Stay with her to make sure she doesn't poke her finger into the blades. But this does work.

In the "good" old days, fevers could go on for months. They were a common symptom of tuberculosis and other contagious diseases fortunately no longer with us. It seemed sensible, at the time, to "force" the fever to its climax so that it wouldn't linger for half a year. The idea, although never medically correct, was popular folk medicine.

It was, and still is, folk medicine for masochistic folk.

AN APPLE A DAY KEEPS THE DOCTOR AWAY

This sounds like an anti-professional plot! I don't want to be kept away. We all have to make a living, you know!

Too bad for the medical profession, but when you get to the core of this myth, you'll find a seed of truth. However, this health advice isn't as useful now as it was in our grandfathers' day.

Sixty to a hundred years ago, it was hard to get fresh vegetables and fruit by the end of winter. They simply weren't available, especially in the northern areas of Europe and North America. The greens were long gone, and there was no transportation or storage available for bringing in greens from more temperate climes.

The one exception was the apple. The apple kept very well in barrels in cold cellars right through to the end of winter. Eating even one apple a day was an adequate source of many vitamins, especially Vitamin C.

Vitamins are the key to the metabolic machinery. Without them, our bodies can't use their fuel efficiently. Even though the old timers had adequate supplies of potatoes for starch and perhaps meat for fats and protein, they had difficulty metabolizing them without vitamins – which the apple provided, in addition to roughage.

One of the most dramatic effects of Vitamin C deficiency was scurvy. You may remember that sailors always had limes on board ship to prevent scurvy. It's true that citrus fruits store better in hot weather, and a barrel of limes would last longer than a barrel of apples on a boat in the South Seas. And, in the tropics, limes would probably be easier to come by than apples. But if you think back to everyone's favourite kids' book, *Treasure Island*, you'll remember that Jim hid in a barrel of apples. Apples, not limes.

Apples were an important staple in Europe and North America. Mostly they were preserved just as nature had made them. But other ingenious methods were devised. Canning applesauce was one. The Mennonites, for example, still make something called an "apple schnitz." You chop up the apple as you would for an apple pie. Then you put the pieces in the oven until they are quite soft, rubbery, and dry. The finished product is delicious to chew on and, in a pie, is indistinguishable from a fresh apple. Not all the vitamin content is preserved in the process, but it's a lot better than nothing.

Apples have lost their paramount importance in our diet. We're fortunate to be able to get fresh citrus fruit all year round. There's no "key" fruit today but the idea of making sure you get your vitamins as a way of staying healthy is still valid. So an orange, or a grapefruit – or an apple – a day may indeed keep the doctor away.

THE ONCE OVER

When you go in for a medical check-up, you can count on the doctor asking you for two things: one is to stick out your tongue; the other is to provide a urine sample.

Look in the mirror, open your mouth, and say, "Ah!" You can't really see much in there because this great big flab of tissue sticks up and obscures everything. The doctor asks you to stick out your tongue primarily to see what may be hiding behind it in your mouth or throat.

The tongue itself has a few things to tell the doctor, it's easier to look at if it's laid out flat. It's hard to see the back of the tongue at the best of times, so this is where the tongue depressor comes in.

Some people worry that a white tongue is a sign of illness. Most tongues look a bit white; but it's just their unevenness and doesn't mean a thing. Unfortunately, a lot of people are scared by the sight of their own tongue and tend to exaggerate its condition simply because they don't look at it all that often.

The most significant thing a doctor can find on your tongue is a sign of cancer. He certainly looks for it, especially if you are a smoker. The sign is usually a reddish, firm, raised area on the tongue, but sometimes it might look like a white spot. Finding a white spot is very valuable because it means the area is pre-cancerous and treatable. Leuokoplacia, or white plaques, are a signal that the area is going to become cancerous. It's helpful to find it at this stage.

Now, passing on to the urine, if you'll excuse the transition. Most samples are disgustingly and happily normal. In the rare cases that one isn't, the doctor usually knows before the lab report comes back that it will be abnormal because the patient exhibits other symptoms of illness during the clinical examination. But urine samples are useful because they are easy, quick, cheap – and the patient thinks *something* is being done. Urine samples are useful for finding hidden infections that aren't showing up anywhere else. Sugar in the urine points to diabetes. Protein in the urine is one of the first, silent signs of a kidney infection which could destroy the kidney if left untreated. So if you aren't complaining of any discomfort but the doctor finds protein in your urine sample, you're way ahead of the game. The infection can be treated before it has a chance to do any damage.

Some doctors insist that your sample be the first urine you pass in the day. I'm usually happy with any sample at all, but there are some good reasons for asking for the first. Because some people will spill protein into their urine only when they're lying down, only the first run after they've gotten up will show it; others passed during the day won't. But that's rare. The other advantage of the first sample is that you've been collecting urine for the seven or eight hours you've been asleep. Whatever is there is more likely to show up then than in urine accumulated only in the two hours since you last voided. However, don't be embarrassed if you didn't catch the very first stream. It's usually not vital.

A medical check-up once a year is a very good idea. Maybe now that you know there's not a lot of hocus-pocus to it, you'll go.

THE CURE

This has been an incredible century in the history of medicine. We have seen smallpox, a terrible plague that has afflicted people for thousands of years, simply wiped off the planet. We have learned to manage killer diseases such as malaria, diphtheria, tetanus, polio, and tuberculosis through immunization and drugs. Surgical techniques have improved to the point that acute appendicitis, the kiss of death fifty years ago, requires only a fairly routine procedure. Antibiotics have turned a critical illness, double pneumonia, into a trivial condition treatable in a doctor's office.

Such stunning successes heighten expectations. We're all waiting for the Next Big Breakthrough. Then a story appears in the papers: "New Hope Found for Diabetes" – or multiple sclerosis or cystic fibrosis or Alzheimer's disease. For the next few weeks or even months, phones ring off the hook at doctors' offices, hospitals, and medical organizations with people asking, "Can you do this for me?" The sad answer is, "No, I can't."

Here's what happens: researchers find that, in a particular strain of white mice genetically prone to diabetes by the age of six weeks and usually dead by three months, it is possible to delay the effects of the disease by one week. This may not be applicable to other mice, let alone other species. They duly publish their findings.

A journalist reads the research paper and follows through by phoning an authority in the field. He asks, "Could this lead to ...?" They indulge in fanciful extrapolation about the potential of the finding. The reporter then writes his story.

The story isn't dishonest. It simply jumps to conclusions. If you read it carefully, you'll see the correct information is all there. But you have to look for the weasel words: "could lead to ...," "may yet mean ...," or "could turn out to be...."

It helps to understand the research process. Was this done in the laboratory or by computer simulation? Was this discovery in an animal? If so, was the animal a special strain and is this non-transferable biology? Although mice and humans share a number of biological similarities, we are also very different.

If the testing was done with humans, was it an initial trial or a confirmatory trial? Initial trials are still a country mile away from licensing and clinical application. There has to be a whole series of trials to disclose any possible complications, a precaution no one is willing to trade off for the intended benefit. Until the story tells you the process or medication is available for licensing and general release, it's not a treatment.

Scientific research isn't always accurate. Some published results have been poorly obtained, and most results are based on statistical probabilities. A statistical probability of one in twenty is considered an acceptable margin of error. When you consider that, although thousands of research papers are being published, only one or two will catch the attention of the popular media, you have no way of knowing how acceptable those two papers are.

There are certain high-profile diseases that always create excitement. Cancer is one. But there's the rub. Cancer isn't one disease – it's a variety of diseases. There will never be The Cure for cancer. There are a few cancers we have learned to cure, others we have learned to manage. But cancers can be as different from one another as a Chevrolet is from a Mack truck, yet they're both automobiles. What is true for a cancer of the uterus isn't true for breast cancer. And even with breast cancer, there are twenty different kinds.

The current big disease is Acquired Immune Deficiency Syndrome. Not a day goes by without an AIDS story in the newspapers or on television. The sociological fallout from this dreadful recent discovery is not only changing our sexual attitudes, but has literally created a plague mentality.

Nowhere is the ability to differentiate between valuable and useless information more critical than in stories about AIDS.

AIDS is truly a tragedy, more so than many killer diseases of the past. There is a significant death rate, but in addition, the wastage of human years is high because it is a young person's disease. As long as it was believed to be only an intravenous drug user's disease or a gay disease, others could turn a blind eye. They no longer can – and they know it.

━━━

AIDS is a very good example of how information can be misconstrued. There are some drugs being used experimentally to treat AIDS patients, but they are not readily available. Reports on their existence have created the beliefs that the drugs are being "withheld." Not surprisingly, black marketeers and other charlatans have stepped into the breach.

There's no doubt people are grasping at straws. They ask, "If the AIDS patients are going to die anyway, why wait until the drugs are properly tested? Why not use these patients as willing guinea pigs?" But the wait is important because, from time to time, you kill more people with the drug or induce more serious side-effects than without it.

There is a real obligation on the part of the medical community, the drug industry and the government that controls it, to demonstrate that the drugs are not going to do more harm than good, that they are not going to shorten people's lives unnecessarily. There is also an obligation to prove that the drugs aren't completely useless, especially if they are expensive, as experimental drugs tend to be.

The individual suffering from the disease may, rightly, feel he doesn't have the luxury of letting science take its lugubrious course. Such conflicts between the individual's needs and the communal good are a serious political issue. The safeguards have been developed to guard us from the possibility of another Thalidomide.

On a more hopeful note, progress has been made and continues to be made. As I read the literature on diabetes, for example, I get more optimistic every year. That doesn't mean help is just around the corner. But it is reasonable to believe that in my lifetime there will be giant steps towards liberating people from the hardships of the disease.

We will continue to search for a solution for various types of cancers. We have already increased survival rates with some. There may not be an over-all panacea, but we are having some successes. The same is true of cardiovascular diseases, which are being managed more effectively through lifestyle changes, decreased smoking and better diet.

The nature of cures is also changing. The focus on drugs and management remains important, but new frontiers are opening up. Biochemical engineering is a distant probability, and gene-splicing for inherited diseases and conditions is a long way off. But you never know when a corner will be turned. For example, we never knew *in vitro* fertilization would be a fact just like that. Research had been going on for a long time and then, suddenly it seems, the process was a reality.

Hope springs eternal, as the poet said, and nowhere more than in medicine. Creating new myths to replace the old isn't progress. Learning to distinguish real possibilities from false hopes is.

—————

Do you have any nostrums you would like to share? I would like to hear from you.

Please write to:

Dr. Ted Boadway
c/o CBC Enterprises
P.O. Box 500, Station A
Toronto, Canada M5W 1E6

Index